Mars Hill Graduate Sch
mhgs.edu/libra

D0190103

CONCILIUM

Religion in the Seventies

WITHDRAWN

Mars Hill Graduate School

10011768

Mars Hill Graduate School Library
mhgs.edu/library

CONCILIUM

EDITORIAL DIRECTORS
BASIC EDITORIAL COMMITTEES: Roland Murphy and Bruce Vawter
(Scripture) • Giuseppe Alberigo and Anton Weiler (Church History)

EDITORIAL COMMITTEES: *Group I: Christian Faith:* Edward Schil-
lebeeckx and Bas van Iersel (Dogma) • Hans Küng and Walter
Kasper (Ecumenism) • Johann Baptist Metz and Jean-Pierre Jossua
(Fundamental Theology) *Group II: Christian Ethics:* Franz Böckle
and Jacques-Marie Pohier (Moral Theology) • Christian Duquoc
and Casiano Floristan (Spirituality) • Andrew Greeley and Gregory
Baum (Sociology of Religion) *Group III: The Practical Church:*
Alois Müller and Norbert Greinacher (Pastoral Theology) • Herman
Schmidt and David Power (Liturgy) • Peter Huizing and William
Bassett (Canon Law)

EDITORIAL BOARD: Johann Baptist Metz • Jean-Pierre Jossua
• Alfonso Alvarez Bolado • Jos Arntz • Paul Blanquart • Henri
Bouillard • Werner Bröker • Daniel Callahan • Bertrand de Clercq •
Joseph Comblin • Etienne Cornélis • Adolf Sarlap • Heimo Dolch •
Albert Dondeyne • Dominique Dubarle • Iring Fetscher • Heinrich
Fries • Giulio Girardi • Jean-Yves Jolif • Andreas van Melsen •
Charles Moeller • Christopher Mooney • Maurice Nédoncelle • Willi
Oelmüller • Francis O'Farrell • Raymond Panikkar • Norbert
Schiffers • Heinz Schlette • Alexander Schwan • Juan Segundo •
Robert Spaemann • David Tracy • Josef Trütsch • Roberto Tucci
• Jan Walgrave • Bernhard Welte

THEOLOGICAL ADVISERS: Juan Alfaro • Marie-Dominique
Chenu • Yves Congar • Gustavo Gutiérrez Merino • René Laurentin
• Karl Rahner • Roberto Tucci

LAY SPECIALIST ADVISERS: Luciano Caglioti • August-Wilhelm
von Eiff • Paulo Freire • Jean Ladrière • Pedro Lain Entralgo • Paul
Ricoeur • Barbara Ward Jackson • Harald Weinrich

SECRETARY: Mlle. Hanny Hendriks, Arksteestraat 3-5, Nijmegen, The Netherlands

New Series: Volume 9, Number 10: Spirituality

EXPERIENCE OF THE SPIRIT

Edited by

Peter Huizing and William Bassett

HEALING AND THE SPIRIT

Edited by

Georges Combet and Laureat Fabre

A CROSSROAD BOOK
The Seabury Press • New York

The Seabury Press
815 Second Avenue
New York, N.Y. 10017

Copyright © 1974/6 Stichting Concilium
All rights reserved. No part of this book may be reproduced, stored in a
retrieval system, or transmitted in any form or by any means, electronic,
mechanical, photocopying, recording or otherwise, without the written per-
mission of The Seabury Press.

Library of Congress Catalog Card Number: 76-26735
ISBN: 0-8164-2096-3
Printed in the United States of America

CONTENTS

EXPERIENCE OF THE SPIRIT

Editorial Note   9

Theology, Charism of the Spirit?   10
  JEAN-PIERRE JOSSUA

Baptism with the Holy Spirit   20
  PIET SCHOONENBERG

Experience of the Spirit and Existential Decision   38
  KARL RAHNER

Blasphemy Against the Holy Spirit   47
  YVES CONGAR

The Spirit and the Discovery of the Truth through Dialogue   58
  LANGDON GILKEY

Mission and the Spirit   69
  BERNARD LONERGAN

Confirmation as the Completion of Baptism   79
  HANS KÜNG

HEALING AND THE SPIRIT

Christian Experience and Therapy   103
  GASIANO FLORISTAN

The Pentecostal Movement and the Gift of Healing   106
  GEORGES COMBET/LAUREAT FABRE

Jesus as a Therapist   111
  HEINRICH KAHLEFELD

What is Healing?   118
  MARIO ROSSI

Healing   124
  ANTONIO MONGILLO

Does the Christian Religion Have a Therapeutic Function?   129
  ALFREDO FIERRO

Contributors   139

EXPERIENCE OF THE SPIRIT

To Edward Schillebeeckx
on his sixtieth birthday

Editorial Note

THE editors and publishers of *Concilium* are pleased and honoured to be able to take this opportunity of offering, in homage to Professor Edward Schillebeeckx for his sixtieth birthday, and as a small tribute to a lifetime's work in exploring theological possibilities and helping to instigate and promote the spirit of Vatican II, a small *Festschrift* within the journal he has done so much to further and to which he himself has contributed so regularly.

The articles, all by noted authorities, concern various essential aspects and topics of Professor Schillebeeckx's own work, and very powerfully complement the themes of the current double issue. They are addressed to nothing less than that unfailing though immensely varied experience of the Holy Spirit that is now engaging more widely the reflective attention of theologians and, in numberless ways, that of a multitude of ordinary Christians, clergy, religious and laity.

Jean-Pierre Jossua

Theology, Charism of the Spirit?

'TO give contemporary man a taste of what he is missing, if only in the perfection of his being — that is the task of the theologian. Anyone who has learned, beyond contingent but objective realities, to recognise the gratuitous, the mystery of those everlasting springs which are inexhaustible but ever close at hand, is a theologian. We understand by theologian one who knows — with the understanding of Sonya, for example, the little prostitute who discovered within Raskolnikov the treasure of life and being, and was able to take hold of it in order to give it back to him. The reader feels that this recovery of buried talent has taken place not merely for the sake of this life, but within the context of transcendence.' That was how Ernst Jünger put it, shortly after the Second World War, in the first chapter, 'Der Waldgang', of his 'Essay on Man and Time'.

This moving text, which comes to us from outside the theological community as we normally understand it, revitalizes us by reminding us of a part of ourselves that we tend to forget. It is more than ever necessary for us to heed its message at a time when superficial writings are proliferating in an alarming way, and in that milieu, at once clerical and academic, where the direct word is all that counts — from the sermon to the scientific treatise — and where the illusion of its effective power remains intact. It reminds us, in fact, that a theologian is nothing without long-standing first hand experience of those sources of life which only spring up from the depths of silence; nothing without a personal language which he creates or can renew if need be, when pressed to reveal himself by describing what he knows, the secret of his life; nothing, unless he is continually aware of the white stone which every person he comes in contact with carries with him; nothing without a heightened perception of the age in which he is living, of its splendid newness as well as of its more distressing aspects and its failures.

As for Jünger himself, there are many indications in the passage quoted, as well as in the context from which it was taken, to prove that there is no question here of that elitism of which he is constantly and somewhat foolishly accused: the last two of these four reminders, for example, and in particular the evocation of Sonya; but also his insistence elsewhere that any man can become such a rebel, a refugee, at the very centre of the urban world, to those immemorial inner forests, when this is the only form of protest that remains to be made, for the common good, against the prevailing violence (let us not forget Hitler, deposed only recently at the time, or Stalin, still gloriously reigning). In the same way, the conjunction of the first point (spiritual experience) and the last (the correct assessment one makes of one's own age in order to serve it) clearly shows that it is no longer a question of purely 'religious' perception, but of an invitation which is addressed (also) to us, Christian theologians, whose task is to bring together interiority and history. In this short work, moreover, there is no lack of references to Christ, to 'that supreme founder . . . who is still, and rightly, the point of reference for our dates, the turning point of time', even while the churches are rejected 'in so far as they are institutions . . . human organisations . . . constantly threatened with sclerosis',[2] and the same is true in *Heliopolis*, written only shortly afterwards. Nevertheless, I do not ignore the fact that certain of the more recent writings show evidence of the fascination that the more primitive forces can hold for the novelist, of a kind of return to the pagan gods.

Our attention has been drawn to a corpus of attitudes which relate to the deepest level of theological activity, to its most necessary conditions and most decisive issues, in so far as it constitutes a preliminary to reflective and critical discussion. To say this and to state, confidently though as yet inconclusively, that theology is a charism of the Holy Spirit is one and the same thing for a Christian. Indeed, for us, all access to the divine world is a grace which comes to us from that same world; for us, all fruitfulness of the word we proclaim or put forward for consideration is derived from that Word which, in the same movement, is there on our lips or penetrates our language; for us, all intuitive awareness of the inner world of other men is a fruit of the charity which alone can hope, against hope, that each one contains within him a potential source of dignity and love; for us, all interpretation of the signs of the times — in the modest sense of the process of discernment to which one subjects the vicissitudes of human life at a given moment in history in the light of the beatitudes, leaving aside all speculation about its progress or its future – belongs to 'prophecy' in the scriptural sense.

Can one leave the matter there, then, commit oneself unreservedly within perspectives outlined by Ernst Jünger – always bearing in mind that economy of grace which in any case would surely not seem entirely foreign to him? Certainly, this portrait of the inspired solitary has a powerful attraction for the theologian in the situation in which he finds himself at present. He is bound to feel upset when he is forced to admit that his word is never heard by urban man. Except of course when, precisely as a theologian, he assumes the role of 'political prophet' in the strict sense of that word, though that in itself is a form of deception because it means presenting a particular ideology in the name of the Gospel, thus doing violence both to the message of Jesus (which cannot throw direct light on a specific political situation) and to the modest, tentative human insights or analyses which get canonized in the process.

He is consequently tempted to become a guru – we are already familiar with various examples of the species, from the inhabitants of the new lamasaries modeled on those in the Christian East or Japan to the shepherd philosopher in the pastures of pure thought – and will point out the freshness of the hidden fountains to those perceptive but rare souls who manage to search him out ... To my mind this particular image of the theologian is paradigmatic of the situation of all who are at present trying to bear witness to the faith at a time when 'mission' is failing and efforts to communicate have reached an impasse, when the ineffectiveness of the spoken word is acknowledged and people are beginning to relearn the value of 'silence'. We Christians are tempted, each one of us, to believe that we will no longer be more than a handful, that from now on the truth is going to be regarded as no more than our personal interpretation of it, that the only responsibility of the gospel witness is to point out to anyone who happens to ask him the direction of the lost path. But if the temptation is the same for all, the arguments which will enable people to overcome it will vary, and at this point we must return to the theologian.

That which we ourselves recognize as the theological charism, and which we know from experience, has nothing whatsoever to do with the vocation of the guru or depositary of wisdom. I have suggested the extent to which we can go along with the definition proposed to us by Jünger – but theology as a charism of the Spirit is not just an unforeseeable gift made in the harsh reality of the times to one whose experience is already rich and deep. We need to characterize it in another way – first from the exegetical point of view and then with reference to the present situation in which we find ourselves – as a service carried out in and for the Christian community. It is the latter as a whole which is in the process of living and reflecting, and doing so for God's sake, for its own enjoyment, and for the benefit of human society. Is there not here a possible remedy for the solitude of the theologian which I described above? Should he not be more concerned to serve his brothers in the faith than simply to become himself a privileged witness to the Gospel? He is no more of a witness than any other Christian — though that in itself is difficult enough, and today more than ever. But the particular responsibility which now weighs so heavily upon him (as it does on the so-called 'missionary priest') he originally claimed and reserved for himself as a form of power. This ecclesial reference of the theological charism is moreover the element that emerges most clearly from a study of the New Testament; the rest is uncertain to say the least.

When one examines the theological charism in the Pauline writings (the major epistles and the so-called captivity epistles) one discovers, as is well known, four lists of charisms (*charismata*): Rom. 12.6-8; 1 Cor. 12.4-11; 1 Cor. 12.28-31; Eph. 4.11-12 (where the technical term is absent but not the gift terminology, *edoken*, which is equally characteristic). In addition there are some complementary passages: 1 Cor. 7.7 on marriage and celibacy as *charismata*, as well as 1 Cor. 13.1-2 and 1 Cor. 14.1 which correspond to 12.31 on the comparison between gifts and charity. The striking thing is that the context of each list is the question of the building up of the unique body (*soma*) of Christ (Rom. 12.5; 1 Cor. 12.12; 1 Cor. 12.27; Eph. 4.12) which is the Church (1 Cor. 12.28) thanks to these gifts which are intentionally different and complementary, and attributed to the Spirit in 1 Cor.

At first sight one might be tempted to think of these charisms as 'functions' (*praxis*, though the meaning of the word is a little doubtful since it is borrowed from the other term of the comparison which is the human body, Rom. 12.4) or at any rate as 'ministries' (*diakonia*, alongside *charismata* in 1 Cor. 12.4, but also used in Eph. 4.12) which are fixed and distinct and define a precise role. This is certainly true of some of these charisms, listed along with the rest, — the term 'apostles' in 1 Cor. 12.28 and Eph. 4.11, for example, in the sense in which Paul uses it has both a more restricted and a wider connotation than 'the Twelve'. But if one examines the lists more closely one notices that most of the gifts mentioned in them are of a less functional nature, and that in addition they are themselves inconsistent (the one gift which is never missing is 'prophecy', also mentioned in the short passage in 1 Thess. 5.19-20). One discovers that even though everyone does not possess all the gifts there is nothing to prevent one of the community from having several.[3] In short, the relationship between more or less exactly defined gift or service and function or ministry in a definite, stable, if not institutional sense is not very clear, and even assuming that the 'theological' charism figures among them, it is not easy to define its exact status in the community: it is a question of establishing first a principle of complementarity to explain the discrepancies and then a notion of organic unity, that is all.[4]

What is more, the lists are fairly inconsistent one with another: it does not look as if they constitute a series of carefully thought out catalogues, each claiming to be exhaustive; and not only that, but the terms they employ do not seem to be always of the same type and as a result either of negligence on the author's part or of ignorance on ours, they remain somewhat indefinite. To demonstrate this one needs only to recall them and at the same time preserve the grammatical form in which they are expressed: prophecy, service, to teach, to exhort, to give, to preside, to exercise mecy (Rom. 12); message of wisdom, message of knowledge, faith, to cure, to work miracles, prophecy, discernment of spirits, tongues, interpretation of tongues (1 Cor. 12.4-11); apostles, prophets, men entrusted with the task of teaching, miracles, to heal, assistance, government, tongues, to interpret (1 Cor. 12.28-31, bringing together v.29 and v.28 for the last term); apostles, prophets, evangelists, pastors and those entrusted with the task of teaching (Eph. 4). Two types of charism are of interest to us here: on the one hand those which correspond to the task of teaching (*didaskon*, Rom. 12.7; *didaskaloi*, 1 Cor. 12.28-29 and Eph. 4) and on the other hand those which produce words of wisdom (*sophia*) and knowledge (*gnosis*), both mentioned and distinguished from one another in 1 Cor. 12.28.

If we stick for a moment to these questions of a general nature, we can ask what is the exact relationship between charisms and charity in 1 Cor. 12 to 14, in order to understand what the concept of 'better gifts' refers to (*ta charismata ta meizona*, 12.31). Charity is clearly not a charism (it is 'infinitely superior', *kath'huperbole*, to the 'better gifts'), any more, indeed, than are faith or hope, both of which also 'remain' (13.13), since as we know the charism of 'faith' in 1 Cor. 12.9 has its own mark, indicated by 13.2. What are these 'better gifts', then, to which we must aspire (*zeloute*, 12.31)? They are undoubtedly the *pneumatika* which must also be desired (same verb) according to 14.1, including, for example, prophecy, which is explicitly mentioned here in contradistinction to speaking in tongues. But if the term is in the plural, one can presume that it also includes the others which figure alongside prophecy in 12.28 in the first part of the list (apostles, prophets, those entrusted with the task of teaching, all mentioned separately) which is divided from the second (miracle and so on, a simple series which ends with speaking in tongues) by an introductory 'then comes' (*epeita*). Let us therefore retain the task of teaching as a charism of the first rank, but without exaggerating the certainty we can claim in this respect.

It has to be admitted that the texts which concern us most directly are no longer particularly enlightening. One can see well enough — taking into account what we know of *didaskalia* and *didaskaloi* from other New Testament sources — what is involved in the activity of teaching mentioned in 1 Cor. 12.28-29 and in Rom. 12.7: doubtless something fairly unassuming. But the status of those who carry out this higher catechetical formation is insufficiently distinguished from the status of those who are responsible for the Church, as Eph. 4.11 bears out: 'finally as pastors (*poimenas*) and men entrusted with the task of teaching', a pastoral role that can be related to 'exhort', 'preside' and 'govern' in other lists.[5] Of course, we know well enough what St Paul understands by 'wisdom', that mysterious plan of God, formerly hidden but revealed today to the *teleioi* (1 Cor. 2.6). But why is it opposed to knowledge? What does *gnosis* mean in this context?[6] How should one envisage the role and task of the theologian, in the sense in which we understand them, on the basis of what is here no more than a directly inspired message? Finally, should one amalgamate the two series in 1 Cor. 12.8 and 12.28, linking wisdom with prophecy and knowledge with teaching? Verse 2 of chapter 13 would seem to advise against this by listing prophecy, understanding of mysteries and of all knowledge, or by including the last two in the first; the same is true of 14.6 which mentions specifically revelations, knowledge, prophecy and teaching. To go on from there, to set them up in contrast to one another, as some do who see the second list as Paul's reply to a Corinthian list, would all the same be to take a step that would perhaps be best avoided.[7]

Thus it seems to me that it would be extremely unwise to search in these texts for the foundation of what theology was to become after Origen, for example, for a criterion for judging it and a source of enlightenment regarding it. And *a fortiori* of that concept of theology as an inchoative science which was to develop, after Augustine, from an intellectualized doctrine of faith according to which the latter (*credere*) is classed epistemologically as 'opinion', inferior to the understanding (*intelligere*) that man seeks; not to mention the efforts made to bring theology into line with modern academic 'sciences'. I even find that at the end of a passage in which he makes a pertinent resumé of what can be said about teaching activity in the apostolic Church, Hans Küng exceeds by a fairly wide margin what is possible to state or even suppose: '*Teachers* are variously mentioned together with prophets. In 1 Cor. they are expressly mentioned in the third place after apostles and prophets . . . they hand on and interpret the message of Christ, and interpret the Old Testament in the light of the young Church . . . Like the prophets, the teachers base their words on the original testimony of the apostles and speak of the present and the future of the community . . . But unlike the prophets, rather than proclaiming intuitively, the teachers *expound systematically*.'[8]

At this point I cannot resist the pleasure of quoting from the Journals of Kierkegaard a passage, certainly not his most ferocious, on 'professors of theology'.[9] I admit that I am tempted to suspect that someone is sure to cite against him, mistakenly, the presence in the New Testament of those who have received the gift of the *didaskaloi*. 'Certainly one can find passages in the New Testament to prove that it is right to have bishops, pastors and deacons (although our own hardly resemble the original model), but then to go on and discover a hierarchy in which professors of theology are mentioned . . .! Why would one laugh in spite of oneself, if in coming to the passage where it is said that God chose some to be prophets, some to be apostles and others to be elders in the community, one were to read in addition: some to be professors of theology? One might as well expect — or almost at any rate — to read: God has chosen some to be government officials! The "professor" is a rather late Christian invention . . . because established round about the time when Christianity was beginning to withdraw into itself, and the high point of the professoral age has coincided with our own time — when Christianity is effectively suppressed. What does the term "professor" signify? The professor suggests that religion is a learned affair; the professor is the most extreme parody of the apostle. To profess what? Something that a handful of fishermen introduced into the world! What an exquisite thought! That Christianity would be capable of conquering the world — that is indeed what the founder himself predicted and what the "fishermen" believed. But that Christianity would press its victory to the point of producing professors of theology — the founder never predicted that. Unless it was when he said that the "apostasy" would come.'

In fact, as I have already said, the only definite point that can be gleaned from this New Testament contribution to the subject is the constant ecclesial reference accorded to all intellectual activity carried on in Christ. The latter is conceived both as a gift of the Spirit and as a form of service, whatever the forms is assumed then and whatever the forms it might assume in our own day. Hans Küng puts it very succinctly, referring to all the gifts of the Spirit: 'The charism relates to the community. The revelation of the Spirit is given to individuals with a view to the common good (1 Cor. 12.7).'[10] In case anyone should accuse us of 'Paulinism', a comparison should be made with 1 Pet. 4.10: 'Dedicate yourselves, each according to the gift (*charisma*) he has received, to the service (*diakonountes*) of one another', where the author gives us as examples 'speaking' and 'service' which are close enough to the Pauline lists.

This is very much our own experience too — and outstandingly so in the case of Edward Schillebeeckx who, throughout the entire compass of his activity, reveals himself as a theologian who is in close contact with people. From his most specialized theological functions — and we all know how concerned he is to maintain his rigorous standards — to his participation in the reflection of 'grass roots' communities, and not forgetting his regular collaboration with the ecclesiastical authorities, he has worked continually to serve the Church in Holland which in its turn has provided him with a real 'space', an experimental milieu, the opportunity — which also serves as a check — to work out his ideas in practice.

Of each one of us theologians, according to his capacity, one could say something of the same. Here I merely want to call attention to one particular experience, to a modest but to my mind genuinely theological task, in which a number of people have been engaged over the past few years, in response to a constantly changing, not to say critical situation in the Church. I mean the task of acting as midwife, in the Socratic sense of the term, to various groups of Christians — groups that may be stable or ad hoc, marginal or fully integrated into the Church, functional (national groupings of larger movements, for example) or friendly and informal, very involved in community action in the city or devoted simply to meditation. This has taught us that it is fairly useless to teach adults academically, and that the same questions, 'resolved' a hundred times over by theologians, keep cropping up again, leading one to suspect that if one has not 'answered' them, it may be because one failed to listen in the first place, and maybe too because one simply has not got an 'answer' — the kind of answer one could nevertheless seek together with them or to which they alone have the key (since politics, sex and the education of children are their affair, part and parcel of their lives . . . as they seldom are of the lives of theologians). But it has also brought with it the joy of helping one of these communities to express what in fact it already possessed within itself, but lacked motivation, self-confidence, technical expertise, sometimes a language in which to express itself (though it might on occasion invent one, and to our advantage), though more frequently the capacity to synthesize and make comparisons; it has meant having the courage to question the group and in good time criticise its procedures; the ability to provide the intellectual tools for further research. the understanding one needs in order to put forward additional suggestions that will be accepted because one has oneself listened and been prepared to learn.

I called it a modest task, but it nevertheless demands far more skill and discipline than one might think, and infinitely more than is required to run a course or give a lecture. The attempt to understand and criticise an experience, interpreting it in the light of the word of

God and the tradition of the Church, brings into play all the resources of theological activity at its most technical,[11] and more especially so since it is not simply a question of 'spiritual' experience — which one must learn, all the same to recognize in renewed forms — but of an experience of the inner confrontation which takes place between faith and a new culture in all its most practical everyday aspects quite as much as in its most rigorous, intellectually speaking, critical instruments.

Experience, a vigorous source of spiritual strength, a coherent understanding of the present — we have returned by another route, via a *maieutics* of the Christian community on the basis of those theological ministries of whose existence we learn in the New Testament, to themes discovered by an independent writer. I will not make the polemical mistake that would lead me on to affirm that within the community the intuition of the individual is preserved, absorbed, while its inherent limitations and the risk that it may be elitist and restricted are avoided. No, although the theologian must not neglect this upsurge of community awareness which is perhaps one of the greatest opportunities for the Gospel in our time — and something that at last gives him a genuinely ecclesial status, though not, however, that of spokesman for authority or party theorist he would also be well advised to learn to appreciate the fragility and the uncertainty of the phenomenon, and above all to remember that nothing will ever replace the personal word addressed to the individual, an appeal to one's contemporaries and sometimes, though more rarely, with the help of genius or the Holy Spirit, a message defying time.

Translated by Sarah Fawcett

Notes

1   German addition in 1951. No English translation.
2   *Op. cit.*
3   Cf. H. Schurmann, 'Les charismes spirituels', *L'Eglise du Vatican II*, vol. II (Unam Sanctam 51 b) (Paris, 1966).
4   At least as regards the extent to which we have chosen to amplify the argument here. For a more detailed assessment of the *Sitz im Leben* of the lists of charisms and their relationship to the various functions, see V. Brockhaus, *Charisma und Amt* (Wuppertal, 1972).
5   Should one discern here a case of development, the merging of things that were originally separate? Cf. H. Schlier, *Der Brief an die Epheser* (Düsseldorf, 1965). For 'teaching' see Gal. 6.6; Acts 13.1; 1 Tim. 4.13; Heb. 5.12; Jam. 3.1.
6   See Col. 1.9; Eph. 1.9. There is no need to insist on the difference between *dia tou pneumatos* (for wisdom) and *kata to pneuma* (for knowledge). Whether or not one should recognize in 'knowledge' a more practical bias, with more room for human initiative, is not clear. On *gnosis* see the book of that title by Dom J. Dupont (Louvain, 1949), now a bit out of date, but still useful.

7   H. Schurmann, *op. cit.*
8   My italics. Hans Küng, *The Church* (London, 1967).
9   *Papirer* XII A 633. See also the rest of the same section, as well as XIII A 122 and XIII A 186. In the last-mentioned passage he suggests what the true task of a 'professor' might be: 'He is able to understand that one cannot understand faith; but this he can do only if his piety is so strong that he can bring to their knees those recalcitrant spirits who are determined not to see this, and who wish, in their arrogance to negotiate with God on terms other than faith, which believes against all reason.' I leave with him responsibility for the expression *contra rationem*, recognizing that it belongs, in his mind, to the category of paradox and is more subtle and more nuanced than might appear at first sight.
10   *Op. cit.*
11   Knowledge of exegetical studies, familiarity with the successive historical factors in which current problems originate, ability to evaluate the effect in one area of choices made in another. I tried to demonstrate this more precisely, for another type of work based likewise on experience, in 'Théologie et experience chrétienne', *Le Service Théologique dans l'Eglise, Mélanges Yves Congar* (Paris, 1974).

Piet Schoonenberg

Baptism with the Holy Spirit

A book that is about the experience of the Spirit ought surely to include some consideration of 'baptism within (the) Holy Spirit'. This term and the reality it denotes have become the focus of attention nowadays because of what is generally known as the pentecostal movement. *Pace* all the distinctions and differences within it, one thing above all motivates the movement as a whole: the conviction that baptism with the Holy Spirit is an event of very great importance and that it can occur in the life of every Christian. It is the foundation for a full 'life in the Spirit' for each individual Christian and for Christ's church as a whole; it is the basis of prayer-life and of missionary witness. In support of this assertion the pentecostal movement appeals to the New Testament, especially the Acts of the Apostles, and to its own experience.

The question as to what baptism with the Holy Spirit entails is a very existential one. For each of us it could raise the issue of whether we are willing to make ourselves open to it. It is a question also for the church as a whole, regarding its inner life and its witness to the world. Now all theological issues are in my view ultimately existential, and conversely, existential questions are not simply clarified but sharpened by theological reflection. That is what has prompted this article. It is an attempt to understand baptism with the Holy Spirit and the question raised for us about that by the pentecostal movement, in terms of the New Testament as well as of the movement itself.

I. THE NEW TESTAMENT

The Term

The English Dominican, Simon Tugwell, has devoted several published articles to baptism with the Holy Spirit, with the laudable intention on the one hand of showing the fundamental importance of what it entails and on the other of dissociating the theology of the subject from a strain of baptism.[1] He starts by remarking that 'in Scripture baptism with Holy Spirit is no technical term'.[2] Yet the verbal phrase 'to baptize with Holy Spirit' occurs in all the gospels and in the Acts of the Apostles. In the fourth gospel Jesus is called 'he who baptizes with Holy Spirit' (*ho baptizon*, 1.33, like Jn. 1.31; cf. Mk. 1.14; 6.14, 24). At all events our term has reference to these New Testament texts and so can certainly be described as biblical. In fact it is pretty well exclusively so.[3]

The passages which speak of 'baptism with Holy Spirit' invariably set this over against the 'baptism with water' administered by John. They are as follows: Mk. 1.8: 'I have baptized you with water, but he will baptize you with Holy Spirit'; Mt. 3.11: 'I baptize you with water . . . He will baptize you with Holy Spirit and with fire' – Lk. 3.16 = Mt. 3.11.

Jn. 1.26, 31, 33a speak of the baptism with water by John. 1.33b: 'He on whom you see the Spirit descend and remain, he it is who baptizes with Holy Spirit.'

Acts 1.5: 'John baptized with water, but before many days you shall be baptized with Holy Spirit.'

Acts 11.16 = Acts 1.5 without 'before many days'.

Thus far the passages customarily cited. Along with them might be mentioned 1 Cor. 12.13: 'We were all baptized with one Spirit into one body, and we were all imbued with one Spirit.'

The words 'with Holy Spirit' are almost always a rendering of *en pneumati hagioi* (only Mk. 1.8 in most manuscripts has simply the dative). The preposition *en* with the dative can be taken here as instrumental, with a certain locative connotation, as for instance 'with/in water' and 'with/in fire'. But the idea of total immersion in Holy Spirit as in the waters of baptism is not altogether obvious in our texts: in that case *eis* is more likely to have been used. Parallel images are more likely present, it seems to me, in the 'will be salted with fire' (cf. Mk. 9.49) and the 'being drenched in one Spirit' (1 Cor. 12.13). That is why in Dutch I have chosen the preposition 'with'. In our texts *pneuma hagion* is written without the article (except where *the* Spirit descends upon Jesus: Jn. 1.32 f); and this I (as opposed to most others) have adopted in my translation. But even part from this absence of the

21

definite article, both the preposition *en* and the parallel with water and fire suggest that 'Holy Spirit' is here regarded not primarily as person but rather as gift (Acts 2.38) and as power (Lk. 24.49). Certainly the Spirit is not the one who baptizes. Who does baptize remains indeterminate in 1 Cor. 12.13; in Acts 1.5 and 11.16 the passive in a Jesus-saying suggests that it is God; in all the other passages it is evidently the one coming after John, the Christ.

Promise and Fulfilment

In Mt. 3.11 and Lk. 3.16 — in the Q-tradition, that is — the Messiah is to baptize 'with Holy Spirit and with fire'; the other texts speak only of baptizing with Holy Spirit.[4] The former are probably the more primitive. It is after all more understandable that 'with fire' should have been dropped at a later stage than added on. Nowhere does the New Testament speak plainly of Jesus as baptizing with fire (ambiguous, perhaps, is the sense of Lk. 12.49 and Acts 2.3). It is in the Q-tradition, therefore, that we are closest to the 'ipsissima vox' of John the Baptist. For him this fire was the fire of the final judgment, which God would enact through his Messiah. This is clear not only from many passages in the Old and New Testaments and the Jewish literature, where judgment and fire are combined,[5] but also from the fact that Matthew and Luke (as opposed to Mark and John) represent the Baptist's proclamation as announcing an imminent judgment. It is even possible that originally the Baptist spoke not of 'Holy Spirit' but simply of *ruach*, wind; for the tempest itself was an image of God's judgment (Isa. 41.16; Jer. 4.11). On the other hand we should not forget that as is clear from its Rule (1 QS 4.13, 21) the Qumran community too looked forward to a purification of each individual at the end: 'He will cleanse them from all evil deeds with the spirit of holiness.' John the Baptist may possibly have taken over the expectation of a final judgment which is to be wrought by fire as well as by the purifying water of that spirit.[6] An objection to this view is that 'Holy Spirit' and 'fire' are so closely interconnected in the sayings ascribed in Q to John the Baptist. Over against that is the fact that in column IV of the Qumran Rule also the emphasis falls on total purification and an end of the conflict between the two spirits, so that there too it is not altogether clear who is to be destroyed and who purified.

However that may be, the Christian interpretation of John's preaching has chiefly emphasized the link between the Messiah and the Spirit. This comes out particularly in Mark's gospel and in John's, where it mentions only 'baptizing with Holy Spirit'. Whereas Q contrasts the Messiah, as the Mightier One, with the Baptist — 'Mightier' being a title assigned to him in particular by reason of his final struggle with the powers of evil (cf. Mk. 3.27 and par.) — the fourth gospel states the intrinsic reason why Jesus baptizes with the Spirit: 'He on whom you see the Spirit descend and remain, this is he who baptizes with (the) Holy Spirit' (1.33). Again it is in this gospel that the Baptist's sayings about the Messiah are most directly focused on Jesus.

At the beginning of each of the gospels, then, stands the promise that Jesus will baptize with Holy Spirit. Tugwell makes much of the surprising fact that Jesus is not thereafter represented as baptizing but — quite the reverse — he is himself baptized.[7] Add to this that the gospel of John sets out to correct the impression that Jesus himself might have baptized during his earthly life (4.1). First of all he underwent a baptism himself, not only that of John but also that of his own death (Lk. 12.49 f; Mk. 10.38 f); and in both instances it was 'bound to be' so (Mt. 3.15; Lk. 24.26). The fourth gospel goes to the heart of the matter: 'Spirit was not as yet there, because Jesus was not yet glorified' (7.39). But what had been promised at the outset of Jesus' ministry was fulfilled in his glorification: he is then the Baptizer with Spirit.

This is not so evident in the gospel of Mark. Only in the appendix to it is reference made to Jesus' activity in his church, actually with an allusion to glossolaly (16.17), but the Spirit is not mentioned. Matthew at the end of his gospel talks about Jesus' universal authority (*exousia*) and his abiding with the disciples; he refers there to the Spirit, together with Father and Son, in Jesus' command to baptize, but does not speak of the Spirit as given by Jesus. Only Luke and John do that. In Luke Jesus speaks at the end of the gospel of 'the promise of the Father' and the 'power from on high', and he will himself send this promise (24.49). We find this reiterated at the start of Acts, followed by a more detailed specification in the words of Jesus: 'John baptized with water, but before many days you shall be baptized with Holy Spirit' (1.5). Here the promise at the beginning of the gospels is clearly associated with the pentecostal event reported in chapter 2 — which furthermore is there attributed to the glorified Jesus himself: 'Exalted to God's right hand, he has received from the Father the promised Spirit and has poured it (or: this) out, as (or: which) you see and here' (2.33). In Acts 10.47 and 11.15 the parallel is stressed between this happening at Pentecost and the Spirit's descent upon the pagans in the house of Cornelius. That too is seen as a baptism with Spirit (11.16). Thus in Luke's theology the promise of this baptism becomes a reality in an event that is not restricted to the Feast of Pentecost but persists beyond it.

The Johannine gospel presents us with the same sort of idea, although the imagery there (probably because of the different layers within the Johannine tradition) is not consistently applied throughout. The words 'baptize with Holy Spirit' do not recur in the gospel. Some affinity with the 'baptizing' belongs to the notion of the Spirit as living water, coming with the glorification of Jesus, probably 'out of his innermost being' (7.37-39; cf. 4.10-14).[8] A fulfilment of that promise can be seen in the water from the side of Jesus dead on the cross (19.34), although there is nowhere at that place any reference back to it and also the texts cited from the Old Testament do not speak directly of the Messiah as giver of the Spirit.[9] Besides that the giving of the Spirit by Jesus is represented under the image of breath, probably even on the occasion of his death (19.20: *paredoken to pneuma*, he yielded up the Spirit) and certainly when, already risen (and ascended into heaven? cf. 20.17), he imparts the Spirit by breathing (upon them) (20.22). This is the Johannine Pentecost, or better: the plenitude of the Johannine Easter, wherein the gift of the Spirit is already included. The various authors of the New Testament try, each one in his own way, to date the eschatological event with Jesus.[10] The Lucan idea of a pouring out of spirit fifty days after the first Easter experience has, according to the agreed opinion of scholars in these days, little likelihood of being in our sense of the term 'historical'. Although Pentecostals may sometimes differentiate between Jn. 20.22 and Acts 2 as two comings of the Spirit to the disciples that are different in character,[11] exegetically this is not justifiable. Rather, these passages give us two representations of one and the same event: the glorified Christ baptizes with Holy Spirit. And just as for Luke so for John this event is not confined to a single day. The five logia on the Paraclete in John 14-16 express the belief that the Spirit continues to be companion to the disciples as 'another Paraclete' (14.16), indeed, 'another Jesus'.[12]

Actual Content

What we have so far discovered is that the promise that Jesus will baptize with Holy Spirit is seen as being fulfilled within the New Testament. In the Lucan theology it is clear enough, in that there is a back-reference to that promise. In John's gospel it is at any rate strongly hinted at. One is tempted at this point to go on to describe baptism with Holy Spirit in the New Testament context; but this is where we come up against the diversity of New Testament theologies. In some writings the Holy Spirit is mentioned only sporadically: in Mark and Matthew, Colossians, the Letter of James. It may be, therefore, that the coming of the Spirit is being described there in other terms, for instance, as the work of the Lord Jesus (Mk. 16.19 f) or as 'Christ all in all' (Col. 3.11-17). Moreover, where the Spirit *is* mentioned or is even the subject of copious discussion, one can point to varying interpretations or certainly to differing emphases. In Acts 2 the disciples are 'filled' ('replete') with the Spirit, and the first result is that they begin to speak 'in other languages' (2.4: *heterais glōssais*), that is, according to the now almost universally received interpretation: in the 'speaking with tongues' or glossolaly which is a gift of the Spirit in other places too (10.46; 19.6). This speaking with tongues is understood by people 'from every nation under heaven' (2.5: Luke here connects the gifts of glossolaly and interpretation). This points to the Spirit's missionary activity, attested throughout Acts as a whole. Speaking with tongues is one – and only one – of the gifts or charismata that in the Pauline tradition are given by the Spirit, but also by Christ or God (1 Cor. 12.8-10; Rom. 12.6-8; Eph. 4.11; 1 Pet. 4.11). Paul speaks of being baptized with the Spirit 'into one body' (1 Cor. 12.13). Thus the charismata are aimed 'at the common good' (1 Cor. 12.7), 'for building up the body of Christ' (Eph. 4.12), for mutual service (1 Pet. 4.11). This is not meant to exclude outward-directed testimony (1 Cor. 12.24 f), but missionary activity is not so strongly linked here with the coming of the Spirit as in Acts. Furthermore there is another strain in Paul to which we must attend. In the Letter to the Galatians the fruit of the Spirit is love in all its forms, accompanied by joy and peace (5.22). In 1 Corinthians Paul combines his conditional recognition of the charismata with his unconditional recognition of love, which he calls the highest gift (12.31). He does not go much beyond a balanced compromise (14.1) – the 'Canticle of Love' (ch. 13) being an interruption of the main argument. At any rate the charismata without love signify nothing (13.1-3); whether there is a more positive connection remains obscure. This dual approach of Paul's to what the Spirit is doing finds a certain parallel in the Johannine gospel. On the one hand it speaks of a birth from water and Spirit, a birth that takes place *anōthen*, meaning both 'anew' and 'from above'. It is an entry into the kingdom of God and a free and surprising gift (3.3-8). Some connection with this new birth may be seen in the authority to forgive sins that the risen Jesus confers on his disciples with the Spirit (20.22 f). On the other hand the Spirit as paraclete is first and foremost witness with the disciples before 'the world' (15.26 f; 16.8; cf. Mt. 10.19 f; Acts 4.8; 7.55, etc.).

So when we try to present an account of baptism with Holy Spirit in terms of its effects, there are a number of different things that we could put in, all deriving from the New Testament. Yet there are some common features that relate to the Spirit's coming (whether designated 'baptism' or not).

(*a*) First of all a full-filling, a repletion, an abundance or superfluity. Acts speaks sometimes of a 'being filled (full)' with Holy Spirit (2.4; 4.8, 31; 7.55; 9.17; 13.9). What is elsewhere said about love and about the charismata fits in with this image of full-fillings: a fulfilling of our inmost being and of our faculties.

(*b*) Next, it is clear from the New Testament as a whole that this full-filling by the Spirit and its intrinsic connection with Christ are a conscious and identifiable experience. We modern Christians so often

25

base our living on a doctrine which we adopt, put into practice and try to make a matter of real awareness. It must have been otherwise with the Christians of the New Testament writings: the preaching (which preceded instruction) had a potent effect on them, they felt the presence of renewed power in their personal lives and in their fellowship. It was something to which Paul could appeal when he wrote to the Galatians: 'Did you receive the Spirit by observing the law or by believing in the message of the gospel? . . . If God gives you the Spirit and works miracles among you, is that because you uphold the law or because you listen and believe?' (3.2, 5). Something must have happened when they took to believing; the receiving of the Spirit must have been a matter of distinct experience. That is why Paul was able to point to the outpouring of the Spirit as a proof of our 'sonship' (Gal. 4.4) and as a warrantable ground of hope (Rom. 5.5).

(c) A related characteristic of the spirit-outpouring is that it affects the body as well. This is shown by the speaking in tongues, the prayer of praise that bursts the confines of our intelligible language, still more so by the cures experienced and the gift of being enabled to serve in that way. The whole embodied person, the *sōma*, becomes a temple of the Spirit, the individual becomes 'one spirit with the Lord', 'the body is for the Lord and the Lord for the body' (1 Cor. 6.13, 17, 19). Thus our ultimate 'spiritual body' is already anticipated (1 Cor. 15.44; Rom. 8.9-11).

(d) As is already apparent, all this is not meant just for each individual personally, it is in aid of 'the body', the church, for its upbuilding. But the gifts, especially in Acts, are also directed to the proclamation of God's great acts to all. The Spirit breaks through the bounds of the Jewish-Christian community and stops Paul from addressing the word to Asia Minor (16.6-10).

(e) Finally, with all this it must not be forgotten that these are gifts for the journey, in expectation still of the day of the Lord, not full to satiety, as Paul makes clear to the Corinthians (1 Cor. 1.7; 4.8). The first Christian communities evidenced the hypocrisy of Ananias and Sapphira as well as the tension between Peter and Paul. In Corinth there were immature people, there was self-esteem and a spirit of faction, and even the Lord's supper was not safe from these influences. The Spirit leads us on the way (Jn. 16.13; *hodègèsei*) to the whole truth and also to true wholeness — and that way is and always was one both of joy and pain.

II. THE PENTECOSTAL MOVEMENT

An Attempt at Understanding

The question now is how the pentecostal movement understands baptism with Holy Spirit. Under the term 'pentecostal movement' I include various groups that subdivide again into three main categories: (a) classic pentecostalism, which appears at the start of the twentieth century and, usually by force of circumstance, exists in distinct and separate churches, for example, the Assemblies of God; (b) the neo-pentecostalism within larger already existent churches: Lutherans, Reformed, Anglicans, that emerged during the 50's; (c) the neo-pente-costalism that in 1967 appeared within the Roman Catholic Church and now calls itself more especially the 'charismatic movement'.[13] The terms 'neo-pentecostalism' and 'charismatic movement' are in any case treated as interchangeable. Both movements are strongly ecumenical in practice. In their theological reflection they part company some-times, because the traditions within which they live confront them with varying issues, in particular as regards the 'place' accorded to baptism with Holy Spirit. The pentecostal movement, under one or other of the forms specified, is to be found wherever Christians are, most markedly in the two Americas. The Catholic version is perhaps most weakly represented in Western Europe, but France is beginning to constitute an exception. It is strongest in North America.[14] I myself have been in touch with it mainly there, through literary and personal contacts.

Of course, for a full understanding of the pentecostal movement one needs to study its history and examine it from a sociological and psychological standpoint as well. More theology is called for too than is offered here. Here I am trying to interpret the pentecostal movement primarily on the basis of my reflection, already proffered, on the theology in the Bible. When one realizes what baptism with Holy Spirit signified in the New Testament, one sees a big difference with the church's life today and indeed for many centuries past. The vast majority of New Testament Christians came to belief through a personal choice, a real conversion. But in our day most Christians (still) are so 'by birth', that is, through the baptism they have received as infants. For the first Christians, therefore, as was stressed earlier on, the actual *experiencing* of the Spirit or of the Lord in their lives was normal and universal. Among Christians nowdays it is certainly not universal and for that reason is hardly regarded as normal. Now like so many revivalist movements all forms of Pentecostalism have this in common: *they look upon this experience as normal and want it to become universal in the Church.*

The intention of the pentecostal movement, therefore, is to be one of conscious and 'felt' Christianity — but not, be it noted, of a super-Christianity. In its Teilhardian sense the term is scarcely understood by the Pentecostals. In the popular sense they do not accept it. They may of course be tempted to see themselves as super-Christians, but their own leaders warn them against that. Here I would like to alert those in particular who do not belong to the movement to that temptation. Anyone who thinks that Pentecostals regard themselves as super-Christians must feel sorry for them (rightly enough, in so far as they have themselves succumbed to the temptation). Anyone who expects them to be super-Christians will be disappointed. They are no such thing. This means, for a start, that they do not represent everything that the Spirit is bringing to life in the churches today. So far there have been no Schillebeeckxs among them, nor any Christians in the mould of Martin Luther King or Mother Teresa. Nor have they discovered the 'theology of liberation' (but some of them are perhaps in their own fashion moving toward practical lines of conduct aimed at liberating others, personally and socially). Again, the Pentecostals do not want to cut themselves off from other people. Their position within Christianity is not that which in its time Qumran adopted within Judaism.[15] If the charismatic movement's periodical in North America is called *New Covenant*, the name denotes the selfsame New Covenant within which *all* Christians live. Pentecostals are no sinless folk, either, any more than were the first Christians. All the sins of Corinth may be found among them, and immaturity in all its various forms. This is something I very much want to emphasize, taking my cue from one of the North American leaders whom I shall be citing presently. For me personally these last points have been of major importance. On first making contact with the charismatic movement in Ann Arbor, Michigan, I was struck by the deep joy evinced by these people. Immediately afterwards I was disappointed when I discovered how a conflict in Notre Dame, Indiana, had been vented in a not so very Christian (rather, a pseudo-biblical) manner. Now I understand that there as elsewhere the Spirit can be really operative, even in face of our sinfulness and immaturity.

What the Pentecostals *are* has been said already: Christians who regard the New Testament experience of the Spirit and the Lord as normal and want it for everyone. But the main thing has still to be mentioned: *they believe they have been given that experience, baptism with Holy Spirit, and they try to live by it.* It is possible that in so doing they understand being baptized with or receiving Holy Spirit in a more precise and thus more limited sense than does the New Testament itself. It is clear already from what has been said that they do not claim to see the whole fruit of the Spirit realized in themselves. They believe first and foremost that they have been blessed with charismatic gifts, and among these charismata three come in for special attention: speaking in tongues, prophecy and healing. Here I shall confine myself to the speaking in tongues. Tugwell considers it more important than a lot of more recent Pentecostals will admit nowadays.[16] It is a capacity for praying out of some deep place within the person, in sounds which for the praying individual himself have no definable meaning. These sounds do not constitute a language which is specific but unknown to the person at prayer, although subconscious reminiscences of other languages can come into play here. The linguo-sociologist Samarin[17] calls speaking in tongues a pseudo-language, a kind of utterance that resembles language in respect of articulation, period-formation and so forth. It is not in itself a consequence of emotional disturbances, nor yet of ecstasy in the usual sense of the word. Speaking in tongues can be simply 'done' by some people, as 'the exercise of a gift', even in a dry and barren spiritual state. It can be both used and abused, for instance, in order to attract attention. In some way or other the contact with God in this speaking in tongues goes so deep that it takes us beyond the frontiers of intelligible language and explicable consciousness. There ought to be an investigation into whether in the course of the church's history speaking in tongues has not been displaced by other manifestations, for example, by the gift of tears, which is the sign of the Spirit with Symeon the New Theologian and plays such an important role, more specially in the Eastern Church.[18] Leaving that aside, I believe that speaking in tongues is one of the expressions of what might be called 'infused prayer'. In the case of the Pentecostals I have sometimes been gripped by the 'whole-heartedness' of their praying – the more so when they have been doing it in their own language rather than 'in tongues'. It is not surprising that Catholic Pentecostals, looking back to their own tradition of spirituality, link speaking in tongues with 'infused meditation'.[19]

The Place of Baptism with Holy Spirit

For Pentecostals, therefore, baptism with Holy Spirit is a coming of the Spirit and with that a being united with Christ, which comes to us as a gift that is experienced and has an abiding effect, particularly in charismata, with the speaking in tongues – or more broadly, infused prayer – receiving special emphasis. As Pentecostals come from a Christendom where this experience is not universal, they are faced with the question of what place to accord it within the Christian life as a whole. It is in supplying an answer that partly at any rate the three currents go their own way. Classic and neo-Pentecostals usually draw a clear distinction between conversion or re-birth and baptism in the Spirit.[20] The Assemblies of God say: 'This wonderful experience is distinct from and subsequent to the experience of the new birth.'[21] Baptism in the Spirit is a 'second encounter', a 'second experience', a 'second blessing'. Sometimes it even comes third, that is, when a further distinction is drawn between conversion and sanctification – which among the neo-Pentecostals, however, is so far hardly the case. The temporal distinction between conversion and baptism in the Spirit

29

is supported from various passages in Acts.[22] I shall not go into the line of argument, firstly because these arguments from Acts are in part open to question and other texts from the same book display the reverse sequence (10.47); then because next to Acts (which some Pentecostals come to regard as a 'canon within the canon'[23]) there stands for example Paul, with whom this distinction is far from obvious; lastly because, even if the whole New Testament made such a distinction, it cannot be tied to a specific theology.[24] Of more consequence is the fact that a lot of Pentecostals nowadays, including Catholics, have had the experience of two distinct crisis-points in their lives. Over against that is the fact that many, of all sorts of different tendencies, have experienced conversion and baptism in the Spirit together. Thus the temporal distinction is no longer so strongly emphasized nowadays. In the Jesus-movements, very largely generated by pentecostalism and the hippie phenomenon, the coincidence of conversion and baptism in the Spirit would seem to be normal.[25]

Classic and neo-Pentecostalism, however, also speak of a qualitative distinction. Although a work of the Spirit, conversion, sanctification or rebirth does not of itself give the Spirit's full presence, which 'fullfills' the whole person. To illustrate this distinction one might turn for instance to Jn. 14.17, where it speaks of the presence of the Spirit 'with' the disciples and 'in' them. This latter, the 'being-present-in', interpenetrates our faculties, which is evident specifically in speaking in tongues, prophecy and healing. For many Pentecostals this means that 'the Spirit' or 'the Lord' takes over our activity, although their theologians, the Protestant ones as well, sometimes specify more clearly the operation of God and man.[26] Wholly consonant with this qualitative distinction is the Catholic-Pentecostal reference to infused meditation or infused prayer. The Stephen Clark aforesaid points to the classic distinction between the way of purification, of illumination and of union. The usual notion, but not the only one, is that these ways follow the one upon the other. Anyone has to go through a whole period of growth before he can come to share the inward contact of the Spirit, giving him the infused prayer. There can however be a different way; and in fact it happens differently in the pentecostal experience. 'The difference between what is happening now in the charismatic renewal and what happened in some traditional forms of spirituality is that in the charismatic renewal, people are being baptized in the Spirit at the beginning of their spiritual growth. Before the charismatic renewal, it was not common for people to experience the gift of the Spirit and infused prayer until some years had passed in their spiritual growth. True, traditional spiritual writers have always known that it did not have to take many years. They knew it could happen at any time. But they did not normally expect it to happen until a person had spent many years in spiritual growth. Now we know that the Spirit can be given freely even to beginners in the spiritual life. This is clearly the way it was given in New Testament times. Many of the people who were baptized in the Spirit in Acts had just heard the gospel for the first time. And the Corinthians and Galatians who were experiencing the many workings of the Spirit had only been converted a few years ago. They were "new Christians". Most of the people in the community I am part of began their spiritual growth only after having been baptized in the Spirit.'[27]

A Few Reflections

Let us for a moment take a look at the passage just quoted, which says very clearly how baptism with Holy Spirit is understood by many people in the Pentecostal movement nowadays and in my view indicates how it may be understood. Not being an American, one soon comes to feel suspicious about the 'instant' gift of the Holy Spirit. In the land of the 'instant breakfast' and 'instant chicken dinner' are the charismata too available for instant consumption, so to speak? The 'sixty-second conversions' found among certain groups within the Jesus-movement reinforce this suspicion. As against that one hastens to repeat that there is no question here of a sort of instantly conferred maturity but rather of a charisma leading toward maturity and holiness. We are not dealing with an 'instant sanctification'.[28] The main thing, however, is that every effort is made to avoid magic of any kind. Every gift of God is possible only through our openness (but the converse is also true). The gift must be prayed for, not just by the surrounding company (whether or not with laying on of hands) but above all by the person hoping to receive it. An express longing and a complete openness are necessary. These insights have induced the Catholic charismatic movement in North America to ensure that about six weeks of instruction and prayer precede a direct prayer for baptism with Holy Spirit;[29] and I assume that other groups have similar practices. Of course there are always temptations associated with a charisma so soon received; but they also go along with 'mature sanctity'.[30]

Another problem has to do with the question whether such a charisma as, for instance, a more ardent, more fervent and thus more deeply-rooted and interiorized prayer-life can go hand in hand with what is on the whole a still immature quality of Christian living. An initial answer is that if we do not deceive ourselves (and so leave a margin for possible pseudo-charismata), this sort of thing does in fact occur. In his First Letter to the Corinthians Paul recognizes gifts that were conferred on them in Christ's kingdom (1.6), while on the other hand he describes their attitude as 'carnal' and childish (3.1-4). That such a thing is not impossible may become clearer when we realize that charismata and

31

virtues are both deeply rooted in man, and yet are not entirely located in the same province. Charismata take hold of our person as embodied, they seem to me deeply rooted in that region of our consciousness and of our physical being which is not yet fully subsumed within our freedom and governed by it. One might regard them as part of our mental-cum-physical *nature*, itself given to our *person* as an advance provision, so to speak.[31] The virtues on the other hand, centred in love, are the response of our free person as such. A concrete example from the sphere of purely human relations is the difference between a deep infatuation and a fully mature love. An infatuation — the experience of 'falling in love' — is not yet the love that brooks no setback or defeat, but it *is* an urgent summons thereto. Likewise infused prayer is not yet a mature love of God (which embraces love of the neighbour), but it impels toward maturity. The comparison between infused prayer and 'falling in love' is not misplaced in that the former also arises as one surrenders to an attraction which is at the same time 'sensuous': the profound humanity of Jesus, the freedom and joy which in his gospel and in a community he evidently sheds upon others, and so forth. Anyone who wants to speak of 'suggestion' here should bear in mind that an element of suggestion is contained in all transference between people. The criterion for a good suggestion is whether it opens a way to real freedom and love, which proclaims its presence in reconciliation, wholeness and a profound peace (as opposed to a superficial gratification: cf. Phil. 4.7).

If we are able to compare the gift of prayer imparted at baptism with Holy Spirit with 'falling in love', another pressing question arises which is important for the Pentecostal movement and for our appreciation of it. Falling in love is a passing experience; every marriage and every friendship passes through a night in which the temptation of parting, of separation, is present, but in which the deepest personal love has to mature.[32] The spiritual writers have shown us in some detail the desert of spiritual barrenness; for John of the Cross our whole spiritual road leads through the night, with only a breaking of the dawn. Jesus was tempted after his baptism, his disciples were not allowed to erect any tabernacles on the Mount of the Transfiguration, but were subsequently made to listen to the predictions of the Passion; Paul admonishes his new Christians, telling them 'that through many tribulations we must enter the kingdom of God' (Acts 14.22). The Pentecostals too are not allowed to forget the temptations peculiar to their situation.[33] One such is the searching after and wanting to cling to the original gift of prayer for its own sake. Josephine Massingberd Ford has wise things to say about the attempt to keep arousing and reviving 'tender feelings of devotion' by means of song, guitar music and hand-clapping. By so doing one can shut oneself off from the Spirit's leading through barrenness to tranquil prayer. What Dr. Ford says is completely in line with the admonitions of Teresa and John of the Cross.[34] After her article in *Spiritual Life* comes one by a Carmelitess, forming a dialectical unity with the one before it.[35] This sister shows that the negative attitude of the aforementioned saints toward emotional expressions of devotion was conditioned by their historical situation and that there are not a few passages, especially in Teresa, where tender feelings of devotion and their expression are valued very highly indeed. So Pentecostals and those who adhere to Carmelite sprituality have things to learn from each other. On the one hand infused prayer need not wait for spiritual maturity, but on the other it will certainly change as we mature and in doing so invites us to mature still further. To come back to my example: with the growth of personal love the condition of 'being enamoured', of being '*in* love', is not really lost, just as a woman's beauty does not have to disappear as she grows older. They both turn into something else, so that there can be a great tenderness about grey hairs and wrinkles. In the same way infused prayer need not be lost, even if tongues and tears vanish away. The very watching and waiting in barrenness can be a charism (if it is a mere feat, it seems to me to be worthless), a continued working and effect of baptism with Holy Spirit.

There is still a final question regarding this baptism and the Pentecostals' whole manner of religious discourse. They strongly emphasize the free gift of God. The Spirit accomplishes the baptism; it is the Lord who baptizes; it is no work of men. J. Rodman Williams says: 'The Spirit comes from without and with mighty impact.'[36] And Clark: 'I always knew that the experience of the Holy Spirit for the early Christians and for the great saints was more than just interpreting what happened to them as the work of the Spirit. It was a distinct recognizable experience.'[37] What can a theologian today say about this experience of God's activity and about the whole Pentecostal way of spaking, in which 'the Lord' does it all? The answer to that question makes it clear that this article not only has something to do with the book in which it appears but also with the person to whom the book is dedicated. Our colleague Schillebeeckx once gave vent, in *De Bazuin*, to his exasperation over the fact that Pentecostals see God everywhere at work.[38] The same Schillebeeckx, however, poses in *Tijdschrift voor Theologie* the same question whether it is really the case that God operates only through his creatures.[39] It is a question that could be put to me, specifically in regard to my study: 'God or man, a false dilemma'.[40] I argued there that God always works by making his creatures work, even in the charismata, the gifts of grace. On the other hand I went to some trouble in the same study to bring out the point that in all this God has the initiative, nay, that he *is* the initiative. I do not mean that I have fully synthesized this latter affirmation with the former one. In speaking about grace I am in fact saying that it is not only mediated by others, but is also given unmediated to a person, for him to mediate it on behalf of others.[41] Schillebeeckx elsewhere speaks of a 'mediated immediacy';[42] and to that I would add: an immediacy that results in mediation. God is never one beside ourselves, as though he were something additional to us. His activity is not competitive, it does not supersede or replace ours. But God's activity must of course be envisaged as 'prior' (though not on a time-scale) or, in more personal categories, as promising, giving, summoning. 'God gives us our activity as that which is proper to us', says Schillebeeckx.[43] Conversely, our activity is also God's gift. In the much quoted work of Rodman Williams this is most often superbly well expressed.[44] To it I would like to add that man does not produce one part or aspect (speech, action), and the Holy Spirit the rest (the language, message, healing power). No, it is all from the human being, but in that human being the Spirit is 'energizing', he is opening up that person to new potentialities in himself. This is an interpretation, but not just an interpretation; for at the base of every interpretation that carries us to God there will somewhere be an experience, albeit in the form of an 'implicit intuition'. But sometimes that submerged experience can become a recognizable experience. I am convinced that with many Pentecostals the experience of baptism with Holy Spirit is authentic, that in their case the Spirit really does speak to men's hearts and makes people whole — just as in this process I would not rule out but would include human psychosomatic factors. I think that the Pentecostals can revive our awareness of God's guidance and leading, even though I am not inclined to exclaim 'Praise the Lord!' with the recovery of every tiny clue. And generally: it is precisely through the demythologizing of the language of the Pentecostal movement that the theologian can be sensitive to what the Spirit is saying through it to the churches (and to himself).

Translated by Hubert Hoskins

Notes

1   Simon Tugwell, 'Reflections on the Pentecostal Doctrine on Baptism in the Holy Spirit', *The Heythrop Journal* 13 (1972), pp. 268-81; 402-14; id., *Did You Receive the Holy Spirit?* (London, 1972). The most detailed study on baptism with Holy Spirit known to me is: Frederick Dale Bruner, *A Theology of the Holy Spirit: The Pentecostal Experience and the New Testament Witness* (Grand Rapids MI: Erdmans, 1970). Bruner says on p. 57: '. . . Pentecostal Pneumatology emphasizes not so much the doctrine of the Holy Spirit as it does the doctrine . . . of the *baptism* in the Holy Spirit.' My own book too is almost exclusively devoted to this subject.

2   Tugwell, 'Reflections', p. 269.
3   In Catholic theology the term *baptismus flaminis* is sometimes employed; but this signifies only the baptism with Holy Spirit that precedes immersion in water (cf. Acts 10.44-48), thus the 'baptism of desire'.
4   For this paragraph cf. E. Schweitzer in *TWNT* IV, pp. 396 f.
5   E. Schweitzer, *loc. cit.*, p. 396, note 417, refers to: Isa. 1.31; 30.30, 33; 31.9; 34.9 f; 66.15 f; Amos 1.4; 7.4; Mal. 3.2; Ps. Sol. 15.2; 4 Ezra 13.4, 10; s Bar. 48.39; Test. Abr. 14; Mk. 9.43-49; 1 Cor. 3.13; 2 Thess. 1.8; 2 Pt. 3.7; Apoc. 20.9; 1 QH 3.28-31; 6.18; 1 QS 2.8-15; 4.13.
6   J. A. T. Robinson, *Twelve New Testament Studies* (London, 1961), pp. 11-27: 'The Baptism of John and the Qumran Community', especially 19 f.
7   Tugwell, 'Reflections', p. 269 f.
8   For the question whether in Jn. 7.38 f Christ is or is not the faithful source of living water, see Raymond F. Brown, *The Gospel according to John, I-XII* (Garden City NY, 1966) (Anchor Bible 29), pp. 320-23. Cf. Hugo Rahner, 'Fumina de ventro Christi. Die patristische Auslegung von Joh. 7.37-38', *Biblica* 22 (1941), pp. 269-302; 367-403.
9   Zach. 12.9-12, however, from which Jn. 12.10 quotes, speaks of a spirit of supplication and repentance, and of a spring of cleansing water.
10   Raymond F. Brown, *The Virginal Conception and Bodily Resurrection of Jesus* (New York, 1973), pp. 111 f.
11   Thus, for instance, Howard M. Ervin, 'These Are Not Drunken As Ye Suppose', Plainfield NJ: *Logos* (1968), pp. 25-35. Erwin dismisses the theory of two versions of a single event with an appeal to the control exercised by the apostles over the tradition. He sees Jn. 20.21-23 as the foundation of the New Covenant, for which reason in Acts the Spirit is no longer given to Israel corporatively, but *is* given to Jews as individuals.
12   Raymond F. Brown, *The Gospel according to John, XIII-XXII* (Garden City NY, 1970) (Anchor Bible 29A), pp. 1135-44: 'Appendix V: The Paraclete', p. 1141: 'Thus, the one whom Jesus calls "another Paraclete" is another Jesus.'
13   The greatest authority in the field of the past and modern history of the pentecostal movement is Walter Hollenweger, author of *Enthusiastisches Christentum: Die Pfingstbewegung in Geschichte und Gegenwart* (Zurich, 1969), and of a nine-part *Handbuch der Pfingstbewegung*, which only exists in a number of typescript copies. A one-volume compendium of this is: *The Pentecostals: The Charismatic Movement in the Churches* (Minneapolis, 1971). See also Bruner, *A Theology*, pp. 19-55: 'The Contemporary Place and Significance of the Pentecostal Movement'. – A history of the Catholic pentecostal movement in the United States is provided by: Kevin and Dorothy Ranaghan, *Catholic Pentecostals* (Paramus NJ, 1969), and by Edward D. O'Connor, *The Pentecostal Movement in the Catholic Church* (Notre Dame Ind., 1971). Half of this last book is devoted to 'theological reflections'. Reports on Catholic pentecostalism, as known to me, are: (*a*) that of the Committee on Doctrine of the Catholic bishops of the USA (1969), see O'Connor, *Pentecostal Movement*, pp. 291-3; (*b*) that of an international conference in Rome, 1973, see *New Covenant* (P.O. Box 102, Ann Arber, MI), January 1974, pp. 21-3; (*c*) that prepared for the Catholic bishops in England and Wales, compiled by Peter Hocken, see *The Heythrop Journal* 15 (1974), pp. 131-43.
14   Catholic pentecostal literature is for the most part in the English language (from the USA and Britain). An exception which confirms this rule is the special number of *Vie Spirituelle*, Jan.-Feb. 1974: 'le renouveau charismatique', in which two articles deal with America and three are translated from English.
15   A cautionary comparison with Qumran is given by Josephine Massingberd Ford, 'Pentecostal Blueprint', *Baptism of the Spirit: Three Essays on the Pentecostal Experience* (Techny III, 1971), pp. 31-77.

16   Tugwell, 'Reflections', p. 408; id. *Did You Receive*, chs. 7 and 8.
17   William Samarin, *Tongues of Men and Angels* (New York, 1971).
18   Tugwell, 'Reflections', pp. 403-5, 408 f.
19   For instance, J. Massingberd Ford, 'Toward a Theology of "Speaking in Tongues" ', *Theological Studies* 32 (1971), pp. 3-29. (This article is also printed in *Baptism of the Spirit*, pp. 79-113.) Stephen B. Clark talks about 'infused prayer' in a passage to be cited later on.
20   See Bruner, *A Theology*, pp. 56-117: 'The Baptism in the Spirit in the Pentecostal Movement'. See too a report on Protestant pentecostalism written by J. Rodman Williams, presented in 1970 to the Roman Catholic Secretariat for Promoting Christian Unity, published in his book, *The Pentecostal Reality* (Plainfield NJ, 1971), pp. 57-84: 'Pentecostal Spirituality', especially pp. 61-68.
21   Cited by Rodman Williams, *Pentecostal Reality*, pp. 63 f.
22   For the discussion about this see: Bruner, *A Theology*, pp. 155-208: 'The Baptism of the Holy Spirit in the Acts of the Apostles: A Comparative Study'; Ervin, *Not Drunken*, pp. 88-104; Stephen B. Clark, *Baptized in the Spirit* (Pecos NM, 1970), pp. 45-58.
23   It is said sometimes – and said with emphasis – that Acts is the only book to give an account of the life of the primitive Church: Don W. Basham, *Ministering the Baptism in the Holy Spirit* (Monroeville PA, 1971), pp. 17 f; Rodman Williams, *Pentecostal Reality*, p. 23, note 5. On the other hand the facts from the life of the early Church are chronicled in Acts about half a century later, whereas the theology of the New Testament letters, in particular the proto-Pauline ones, stands closer to and is affected by the Christian experience.
24   It is important to notice that the gift of the Spirit, associated with laying on of hands and prayer by the apostles sent from Jerusalem (Acts 8.14 f), probably prevented the forming of a splinter-group and certainly allowed expression to the Christian healing of the Samaritan schism. Here and elsewhere, where the encounter with Christ and reception of the Spirit are in point of time really quite separate, Luke makes much of the prayer that precedes the latter (Aacts 1.14; 9.9, 11), as between Jesus's baptism and the descent of the Spirit upon him (Lk. 3.21).
25   See *The Jesus Kids and their Leaders*.
26   See for instance: Rodman Williams, *Pentecostal Reality*, p. 12.
27   Clark, *Baptized*, pp. 67 f.
28   Rodman Williams, *Pentecostal Reality*, p. 12. Cf. O'Connor, *Pentecostal Movement*, pp. 171 f: 'No Instant Sanctity'.
29   *Team Manual for the Life in the Spirit Seminars*, completely revised, ed. Stephen Clark, Notre Dame Ind.: Charismatic Renewal Services.
30   I read somewhere this remark of a French religious about one of her fellows: 'Elle aura un long purgatoire à cause de ses vertus.' The perhaps most profoundly empathetic description of the subtle temptation of heroic virtue is given by Gertrud von le Fort in her short story, *Die Letzte am Schafott*.
31   I borrow this distinction between nature and person from Karl Rahner, particularly in: 'Zum theologischen Begriff der Konkupiszenz', *Schriften zur Theologie* I (Einsiedeln, 1954), pp. 377-414.
32   J. Walgrave, 'Dialectiek van het huwelijk', *Kultuurleven* 25 (1958), pp. 165-76.
33   Donald Gee, *Temptations of the Spirit-filled Christ* (Springfield MO, 1966). Christ's temptations in the wilderness, in Luke's sequence, are: selfishness, compromise, fanaticism.
34   J. Massingberd Ford, 'Fly United – But Not In Too Close Formation: Reflections on the Catholic Pentecostal Movement', *Spiritual Life* 17 (1971), pp. 12-20. See too her article: 'Tongues – Leadership – Women: Further Reflec-

tions on the Neo-Pentecostal Movement', *ibid.*, pp. 186-197. A piece of critical reflection also deriving from Notre Dame itself is to be found in Henri Nouwen, *Intimacy* (Notre Dame Ind., 1969), pp. 77-90: 'Pentecostalism on the Campus'. As a matter of fact, O'Connor too points out the danger of 'Charismania' and 'Paraclericalism': *Pentecostal Movement*, pp. 225-231.

35   Teresa del Monte Sol, 'Pentecostalism and the Doctrine of Saint Teresa and Saint John of the Cross', *Spiritual Life* 17 (1971), pp. 21-33. Cf. O'Connor, *Pentecostal Movement*, pp. 210-215.

36   Rodman Williams, *Pentecostal Reality*, p. 14. But see note 26 above.

37   Clark, *Baptized*, pp. 8 f.

38   E. Schillebeeckx.

39   E. Schillebeeckx.

40   P. Schoonenberg, *Hij is een God van mensen* ('s-Hertogenbosch, 1969).

41   P. Schoonenberg, *God van mensen*.

42   E. Schillebeeckx.

43   E. Schillebeeckx.

44   See above, note 26.

Karl Rahner

Experience of the Spirit and Existential Decision

THE author of this short article has on numerous occasions in the past given his views on subjects which would fall very easily under this title. As a result, he does not know whether he really has anything new or fresh to say on the matter. But 'spiritual experience' is the subtitle of the *Festschrift* for Edward Schillebeeckx, and so he comes back to his old theme in an effort to say something different, or at least clearer and more complete.

Looked at more closely, the subject is indeed endless. Almost at first sight it turns out to be little more than another version of the topic of 'transcendence and history'. There is a difference, however. To say this we must be clear, as current seminary theology has for a long time not been, that the gift of the divine Spirit as such, even in a true self-communication of God, takes place primarily in man's transcendental nature. It does not take place in an inner or outer categorial reality of man and his consciousness, as though these served as the material for free human decisions. Obviously, however, 'transcendence and history' can neither be properly discussed here nor assumed to have been defined in all its aspects, and we must therefore make a reservation with regard to our real subject. On this we can only make two observations; they will rapidly lead into darkness, and we shall be unable to follow them to a conclusion.

Some peculiarities of an existential decision must first be noticed. They are peculiarities of particular importance to our present concerns, and should not create the impression that we are offering a complete description of the nature of an existential decision. By an existential decision we mean (and we are staying within Christian theology) an act of human freedom in which a person possesses ultimate control over himself before God. Ultimately it is unimportant whether this 'before God', i.e., the acceptance or rejection, is or is not made explicit and verbalized in the decision. On the one hand real freedom in relation to a categorial object and a finite value (or one conceived as finite) is not possible without a transcendental reaching out towards absolute Being and the absolute Good (this seems obvious to the Thomist). On the other hand, in the same measure every genuinely free decision involves — explicitly or not — a relation between a free subject and God. It is ultimately the actualization not only of a free attitude to the explicitly given categorial object on which historically constituted freedom always bears and by which it is mediated to itself, but also of a freedom in relation to the transcendental horizon of freedom, in relation to its unrestricted reaching out towards the absolute Good and God.

This at least is a basic conviction of the Christian view of man. Christianity holds that man is free in relation not only to the categorial and finite object of his free choice or to the concept of God in his objective consciousness, but also in relation to God himself. The transcendental nature of freedom does not simply make possible a *categorial* choice (which God, as the guardian of the law of God which we conceive of in conceptual terms, subsequently provides with additional intellectual constructions with moral implications), but the true object of freedom. Categorially limited action does not just take place against the horizon of a transcendence which is open to the absolute, but changes this horizon itself. It changes it so radically that one possible, freely established state of this transcendence has to be called salvation, the free acceptance of God's self-communication, and the other state absolute damnation, the permanent failure to rise to this self-communication of God.

An explanatory note is necessary here. We realize that in talking in this way we are talking about human transcendence as raised to a higher level by grace, which orients it to the pure immediacy of God. There is a legitimate limiting concept of 'mere nature', a transcendence in knowledge and freedom which cannot promise or claim to provide complete union with the goal of man's unlimited transcendence, which is always sought after but never reached. This, however, is really a limiting concept, and it is illegitimate to use it as the basis for any arbitrary deductions about the nature of man. However much the explicit concept of a transcendence exalted by grace may be a concept of Christian revelation, this does not mean that theoretically (rather than as a matter of history) it can only be experienced within the explicit Christian revelation. Let us allow that a spiritual experience, in the Christian sense, may take place outside conscious, explicit and institutionalized Christianity. If this experience of the Spirit, wherever it occurs, is already a genuine occurrence of revelation, what is meant by 'graced transcendence' is still a part of revelation. If so, it is most fully and accurately described within explicit Christianity, and arguably derives greater general conceptual clarity from Christianity. 'Graced transcendence', however, is a concept which should be introduced into philosophical anthropology only very cautiously and with the support of positive theological data. Wherever unlimited transcendence appears, wherever the courage to face this limitlessness is unchecked and a person surrenders himself without reserve to the existing absoluteness of his transcendental nature, there he experiences that transcendence which, when enriched by grace, leads to the immediate presence of God. This is true whether the process is conscious or not, whether the individual can explain it to himself in these terms or not. It is true even without reference to the theory which has as a matter of fact been developed in what Christians call the explicit history of revelation.

This free control in an existential decision (for acceptance or rejection) over human transcendence ennobled by grace is always exercised on historically finite, categorial material. It is in this material that freedom is actualized and the subject mediated to himself.

What relation is there between freedom as freedom in relation to the categorial object and freedom as the subject's freedom in relation to himself, and so also to God? It is very complex. It is a fact, though not so inherently obvious as is generally thought today, that there can be technically wrong individual decisions which do not break a person's positive relationship with God, the so-called 'objectively' sinful but 'subjectively not culpable' sins. This shows that there is no absolutely fixed relation between the categorial content and the transcendental significance of a decision in freedom. The 'content' of such a decision, of course, here means the explicitly stated, expressed object and the empirically and historically accessible and intellectually determinable stuff of such a decision. It does not include the transcendental element of consciousness in such an act which is not only always present but also in relation to which this discrepancy between the judgment of such an act by God and in the sight of God and the way it appears to the agent is naturally impossible. This means, however, that the modification mentioned above with the categorial decision produces in the grace-enriched transcendental consciousness is not always related, or does not have a clearly determinable conscious relation, to this categorial content. This is also implied by the Catholic teaching that no-one can 'judge' himself with absolute certainty, can know with total certainty whether he is in a state of grace or assess with complete assurance another person's relationship to God. Our explicit verbal understanding of human transcendence as enhanced by grace (the only form in which we can bring it to bear on a conscious decision) cannot be a basis for deducing a particular object of choice, since such an object is always distinct from the goal of grace-enhanced transcendence. The converse is also true (if it were not, the previous statement would be false), i.e. a particular categorial object of choice, even when it is technically correct, that is, conforms to the objective structures of man and the world, is still not conclusive proof that its choice establishes a positive relationship to human transcendence and its goal.

Purely as an aside, it may be mentioned that this would be a good place to start a discussion of the question whether a substantive specifically Christian morality exists or not. But we cannot discuss it here.

We have now reached our real subject, but before describing it in more detail we must say something about the second term in the title of this article, spiritual experience in itself. We are going to put forward a thesis which there is no room to argue in detail here, simply as a premise. It is that authentic spiritual experience in its essential nature does not entail an individual object of experience within the domain of consciousness. It consists, rather, we would argue, in the experience of the radicalization by grace of human transcendence (in knowledge and freedom) which turns it towards to immediacy of God. This is brought about by the self-communication of God to the spirit which receives grace. Spiritual experience (we leave for later the question whether freedom accepts or rejects this experience) is not the result of a single action of God 'from outside' on the human spirit regarded as definitively constituted. It means that God, through his self-communication ('uncreated grace'), becomes always and everywhere in grace a co-constitutive principle of the human spirit in its transcendence. Spiritual experience is experience of the every-present radical quality of human transcendence, which goes beyond itself towards God-in-himself because it is always supported by God's self-communication. This deepest radical quality of human transcendence may be present in man as 'nature', in the form of free acceptance, or in the form of rejection and defiance. (In the first possibility 'nature' refers to everything which is a condition of the possibility of the existential self-possession which constitutes human freedom, irrespective of whether it is simple, finite created reality or only related to such a reality — the 'essence' of man — and in its own way a free gift.) Like every other experience, this transcendental experience of the radical quality of the Spirit as a result of the self-communication of God is mediated by a categorial object, because the finite spiritual nature of man only comes to awareness of itself by coming to rest in another, and it may be remarked in passing that this other is always ultimately personal. This, at least, is the normal state. We ignore the question whether a mysticism is conceivable in this life in which this transcendental experience of the enhancement of the spirit by grace can really take place without the mediation of a categorial and *a posteriori* object from outside. Naturally even this transcendental experience can always be objectified, as in the present discussion. It can in this way always become a particular object within human consciousness. Nonetheless the transcendental experience itself and its conceptualizations are not the same thing and should not be confused, nor should we tolerate the tacit assumption that this transcendental experience radicalized by grace is only present when its conceptualizations are present in the form of categorial objects or when the transcendental experience is represented in consciousness by an explicitly 'religious' object. This is all we can say here about one basic assumption of our discussion. The thesis stated is based ultimately on the realization that every categorial object and every experience of such an object is finite, and that among such categorial objects, whether in a particular case their existence is caused by God or something else, there can be no absolutely essential distinction which would allow some to be seen as specially and directly the result of God's action and would deny this status to others. To maintain the opposite is ultimately to have a mythological view of the relation between God and the world.

We now come to our real subject: what is the relation between experience of the spirit and existential decision? When we talk about an existential decision in this context we mean one which chooses a particular cateogrial object, such as a specific career, a particular course of action towards another human being, contracting a marriage, performing a particular categorial religious act, etc. Naturally, an existential decision should always also be the expression of a fully specific relationship to the person's existing grace-enhanced transcendence and so to God in himself, but this in turn raises the question of the precise relationship of the choice of a categorial object in an existential decision, the acceptance or rejection of the God who offers himself in self-communication as the ultimate force of our transcendence, giving our transcendence as such its actual form in freedom. This relationship clearly presents a very obscure problem. As already mentioned, the choice of a categorial object can be objectively wrong and yet the expression of a positive relationship to God. Equally on the other hand, the fact that the object chosen is objectively correct for that person by this-worldly standards, that it lies within the domain of the positive norms established by God, does not in itself mean that choosing it establishes a really positive relationship to God in his authentic self-communication. The reason why this does not follow is not just that psychological freedom of choice and its exercise in relation to a categorial object does not simply coincide in every case with an authentic existential determination by the subject of his life. (If it did, the idea of a 'venial sin' *ex imperfectione actus* and its positive counterpart, an act involving only a 'slight exercise of freedom', would be nonsense.) There is another reason why the choice of an object correct in this-worldly terms does not of itself guarantee that the existential decision has been correctly made. The existential decision has to do with transcendental spiritual experience and with God, whereas clearly in an existential decision it may happen that several categorial objects present themselves to freedom to be chosen in a particular situation. Of themselves, all may appear to be objectively more or less equally possible, and yet only one of them can be chosen as willed by God, i.e. chosen at this moment as the necessary actual material of a positive attitude to spiritual experience and an existential relationship with God. Naturally, the view that in a choice between several objectively correct (good) objects the decision has an importance of its own for the relationship with God is not simply obvious. We follow this view here as the conviction of those who practise a genuine spirituality and have been convinced by it that God's will in the particular case, while it may include and presuppose the objective rightness of an act (its conformity with 'God's commandments', with human nature, the nature of the Church, etc.), is nevertheless not in itself adequately defined by all this. Naturally this view is perfectly compatible with the hypothetical case in which, in relation to God, the choosing subject is to some extent thrown back on to the indifference of objects of choice which is in any case inherent in human freedom. This also makes it impossible to appeal from the spiritual experience just adduced to a different sort of experience, since the latter could be explained as just this hypothetical case and so would be no argument against the view that a choice between objectively good objects must involve reference to God.

But how are we to imagine such an existential decision? It has to choose between good objects, not arbitrarily but by means of a choice made by God, and so with reference to God. The ordinary simple believer will generally have no great problem here, nor should he be disturbed in this simplicity. He feels that when he has to make such a choice God 'tells' him which of the possible objects to choose. He feels that God 'enlightens' and 'inspires' him so that he knows for certain what 'God's will' is in the particular case. But it is not really possible to imagine the choice of the right object for a particular time and place as resulting from an identifiable intervention of God's. This would be to claim a 'private revelation', and even in the highest decisions in the life of the Church theology allows no 'new revelations'. Nor is it any good claiming that our case involves 'only' the private area of human life, since this is really just as important as the 'public' religious life of the Church. And even if we were prepared to consider a private revelation possible, it could not be an essential condition of all the decisions considered here.

What then, in an existential decision, can be the basis for choice between a number of objects all more or less equally justified by the objective moral law but only one of which can be willed and ordained 'by God'? If it is possible to give such a description of an existential decision in the circumstances mentioned without explaining it in mythological terms, it can only be done by a synthesis of the transcendental spiritual experience and the encounter with the categorial object which is always present to freedom in a particular situation.

We are trying to imagine a synthesis in which one morally possible object is experienced as destined for us by God in preference to others. First, however, we must consider a different point. Transcendental experience of God as a result of his self-communication in grace is not experience of a thing, or simply of a necessary being, but of a free personal reality. It is to this reality that we give ourselves when we surrender to the God present in necessary transcendental experience in the freedom of our own faith, hope and love. Where human freedom is exercised it experiences itself (explicitly or inexplicitly) as a gift from the free God and a continuation of God's creative act into the essential activity of the creature, which is constantly dependent on God, not merely in its substantial being, but also in its free activity. In these terms such a synthesis of transcendental and categorial is perfectly conceivable. The categorial object willed in freedom can quite well be seen as creatively imposed by the freedom of God.

This is all very well, but how does it enable us to understand the particular 'synthesis' of transcendental and categorial in and through which the one *choice* possible in relation to God is turned into a choice between different objects? One possible answer is that a synthesis which implies such a choice is at least not excluded where the categorial object does not conceal or exclude transcendental experience, but allows it and probing consideration of it to exist undiminished. Even this is not simply obvious, merely because the categorial object of choice is assumed to be morally positive and capable of being chosen on purely human grounds. On the other hand we are quite familiar with the situation in which, for a particular person, one or other possible object of choice, though morally positive, simply will not enter freely and unimpeded into that movement of human knowledge and freedom which is the substance and the meaning of transcendental spiritual experience. The thoughtful person, who goes to norms and general principles and measures an object of choice by them, can find no theoretical objection to the choice of a particular categorial object, but it does not appeal to him. It checks and obscures the free rise of the transcendental spirit, in contrast to another object of choice, which does not produce this experience of restriction and darkness. It is also possible for a number of objects of choice to offer themselves in a similar way to this synthesis with none of them obscuring the spirit's transcendental experience. In this case all these objects are possible in the sight of Hod and not just in terms of this-worldly rationality, and the will of God really favours this free choice between these objects for its own sake and not a particular object. Whatever object happens to be chosen in such a situation has no more significance for spiritual experience or in relation to God than any other object which might have been chosen.

It is possible (and indeed necessary) for the synthesis willed by God between the particular categorial object of choice and the transcendental spiritual experience to be experienced also in a more positive way. It may happen that the freely accepted transcendental experience of the spirit is here and now impossible in any other way than through a free turning to the particular one of several objects of choice. This object then not only does not lessen or distort the spirit's experience, but transmits it positively as its only possible channel in this time and place. By the terms of what was said above, it is possible for what is by secular standards not an objectively correct object of choice (one which does not conform with the norms of the moral law) to mediate in practice the free acceptance of transcendental spiritual experience. However, it is clear that where this this-worldly perversity is given a positive value and actively desired, there can be no experience of a synthesis between transcendental spiritual experience and a categorial object of choice. The opposite assumption would entail that the will of God as creator had fundamentally no relation at all to the structures of the created world, but maintained an attitude of indifference to them. In fact, though, transcendental experience fundamentally includes the will of God for his world. Where therefore what in this-worldly terms and here and now was really perverse was consciously and freely chosen, and an attempt was made to reach a synthesis between a perverse categorial object and a freely accepted transcendental spiritual experience in this way, this will would be equivalent to an absolute rejection of spiritual experience. Such a synthesis is impossible.

What has been said above is no more than a very abstract and general outline of how and why spiritual experience and an existential decision about a particular object are bound together and affect each other. It would certainly have been possible to give a much clearer detailed description of what we have tried to talk about here. But we can say no more here about the psychology of transcendental spiritual experience in grace or about a logic of existential decision which cannot be reduced to the logic of theoretical reason. Nor can there be any appeal here to the evidence of the theological tradition, which bears witness more or less clearly to this unity between the transcendental experience of the free spirit (of both God and man) and existential decision. In particular we could not, and chose not to, make explicit reference to the *Exercises* of St Iganous of Loyola. This would have meant entering still unsettled controversies about the interpretation of the texts, which in our view support the thesis of the unity of spiritual experience and existential decision. But if anyone is tempted to think that what has been said in this short article is all empty speculation and theory-spinning, with nothing to do with the actual reality of human life, they must face a number of questions. Do they, for example, allow sufficiently for the distinction, which definitely exists, between inexplicit transcendental experience occurring around a specific object of consciousness but nevertheless without forming a categorial object for itself, and an explicit, objectifying and verbalizing concept of such a transcendental experience? The second form may not generally be present in ordinary life, but that by no means implies that transcendental spiritual experience is itself absent. Another question is this. If someone wanted to maintain that they never experience this synthesis between transcendental spiritual experience and an object of an existential decision, they would have to say whether they believe it to be necessary, for the views put forward here to be correct, that syntheses of this sort should often be present in life or experienced with any degree of conscious clarity. Is it not also conceivable that such genuine fundamental choices and decisions, to the extent that they can be localized at all in time and space, are relatively rare and even so determine the rest of human life?

Translated by Francis McDonagh

Yves Congar

Blasphemy against the
Holy Spirit

(Mt. 9.32-4; 12.22-32; Mk. 3.20-30; Lk. 11.14-23; 12.8-10)

LET us first set out these texts in synoptic form. The translation is
that of the Jerusalem Bible:

Mk. 3.20-30	Mt. 9.32-4
20.He went home again, and once more such a crowd collected that they could not even have a meal. 21. When his relatives heard of this, they set out to take charge of him, convinced he was out of his mind.	
	32.They had only just left when a man was brought to him, a dumb demoniac. 33.And when the devil was cast out, the dumb man spoke and the people were amazed. 'Nothing like this has ever been seen in Israel' they said. 34.But the Pharisees said, 'It is through the prince of devils that he casts out devils.'
22.The scribes who had come down from Jerusalem were saying, 'Beelzebub is in him' and, 'It is through the prince of devils that he casts devils out'.	
23.So he called them to him and spoke to them in parables, 'How can Satan cast out Satan?'	

Mk. 3.20-30 **Lk. 11.14-23**

24. If a kingdom is divided against itself, that kingdom cannot last.
25. And if a household is divided
against itself, that household can
never stand.
26. Now if Satan has rebelled against
himself and is divided, he cannot
stand either — it is the end of him.

27. But no one can make his way into
a strong man's house and burgle his
property unless he has tied up the
strong man first. Only then can he
burgle his house.

28. 'I tell you solemnly, all men's
sins will be forgiven, and all their
blasphemies; 29. but let anyone
blaspheme against the Holy Spirit
and he will never have forgiveness:
he is guilty of an eternal sin.'

Mt. 12.22-32

22. Then they brought to him a blind
and dumb demoniac; and he cured
him, so that the dumb man could
speak and see. 23. All the people
were astounded and said, 'Can this be
the Son of David?'
24. But when the Pharisees heard this
they said, 'The man casts out devils
only through Beelzebub, the prince
of devils'.

25. Knowing what was in their minds
he said to them, 'Every kingdom
divided against itself is heading for
ruin; and no town, no household
divided against itself can stand.
26. Now if Satan casts out Satan, he
is divided against himself; so how can
his kingdom stand?
27. And if it is through Beelzebub
that I cast out devils, through whom
do your own experts cast them out?
Let them be your judges then. 28.
But if it is through the Spirit of God
that I cast devils out, then know that
the kingdom of God has overtaken
you.

14. He was casting out a devil and it
was dumb; but when the devil had
gone out the dumb man spoke, and
the people were amazed.

15. But some of them said, 'It is
through Beelzebub, the prince of
devils, that he casts out devils'.
16, Others asked him, as a test, for a
sign from heaven;
17. but, knowing what they were
thinking, he said to them, 'Every
kingdom divided against itself is
heading for ruin, and a household
divided against itself collapses.
18. So too with Satan: if he is divided
against himself, how can his kingdom
stand?
— Since you assert that it is through
Beelzebub that I cast out devils. 19.
Now if it is through Beelzebub that
I cast out devils, through whom do
your own experts cast them out?
Let them be your judges then. 20.
But if it is through the finger of God
that I cast out devils, then know that

48

Mt. 12.22-32

29. 'Or again, how can anyone make his way into a strong man's house and burgle his property unless he has tied up the strong man first? Only then can he burgle his house.

30. 'He who is not with me is against me, and he who does not gather with me scatters.

31. And so I tell you, every one of men's sins and blasphemies will be forgiven, but blasphemy against the Spirit will not be forgiven. 32. And anyone who says a word against the Son of Man will be forgiven; but let anyone speak against the Holy Spirit and he will not be forgiven either in this world or the next.

Lk. 11.14-23

the kingdom of God has overtaken you.
21. So long as a strong man fully armed guards his own palace, his goods are undisturbed; 22. but when someone stronger than he is attacks and defeats him, the stronger man takes away all the wespons he relied on and shares out his spoil.
23. 'He who is not with me is against me; and he who does not gather with me scatters.'

Lk. 12.8-10
8. 'I tell you, if anyone openly declares himself for me in the presence of men, the Son of Man will declare himself for him in the presence of God's angels. 9. But the man who disowns me in the presence of men will be disowned in the presence of God's angels. 10. 'Everyone who says a word against the Son of Man will be forgiven, but he who blasphemes against the Holy Spirit will not be forgiven.'

The verses referring to blasphemy against the Holy Spirit are rightly considered difficult to interpret. St Augustine said of them: 'In omnibus Sanctis Scripturis nulla maior questio, nulla difficilior invenitur.'[1] I do not propose to examine the history of the exegesis here, though I have done so elsewhere, either on the basis of J. Knabenauer,[2] or through my own researches. I have of course taken account of recent studies.[3]

The texts speak of blasphemy, which means a word against a sacred reality that contains a divine quality. Many authors speak of the sin against the Holy Ghost, or go from blasphemy to sin. This is because this blasphemy is a sin, of which it is said that there is no forgiveness, and no remission: 'He will never have forgiveness; he is guilty of an eternal sin.' But this sin is that of having blasphemed, not against the Son of Man, but against the Holy Spirit. According to the Judaic law established in Leviticus, blasphemy against God was punished by death.[4]

This pericope has no parallel in John, except perhaps the allusion in 1 Jn. 5.16-17, which we shall come back to in due course. The three synoptics present the passage in different ways: in Mark, unlike Matthew and Luke, his family are convinced he is out of his mind. Mark also has it that *all* sins and blasphemies will be forgiven except blasphemy against the Holy Spirit; he does not refer to blasphemy against the Son of Man, and this cannot be implied because blasphemy against the Spirit is explained by the fact that the scribes who came from Jerusalem claimed that Jesus had an impure spirit and cast out devils by the prince of devils. This blasphemy is therefore aimed at Jesus, not the disciples or the Church. The 'he who is not with me' in Matthew and Luke figures elsewhere in Mark — 9.40 — and in a different form. But in Mark this pericope comes immediately after the calling of the twelve, to whom Jesus gave the power to cast out demons, so that the application of the blasphemy to Jesus himself as sovereign exorcist is open to application to the disciples and the Church.

For various reasons, Lagrange and Manson in their commentary, Bultmann, H. B. Swete and H. Leisegang all consider Mark's version to be the most ancient and authentic.[5] But according to Leisegang, it is not the Spirit in the mouth of Jesus that is meant: Jesus drove out devils by the name of God, not by the Spirit, so in blaspheming against Jesus, the scribes were blaspheming against the name of God . . . but this idea has met with general criticism.[6]

What is common to Matthew and Luke and not found in Mark is generally attributed to Q: the occasion of the confrontation, i.e. the healing of the dumb demoniac, Jesus' claim that he casts out devils through the Spirit of God (Mt.), or the finger of God (Lk.), which means the coming of the kingdom of God, and finally the affirmation

of the difference between speaking against the Son of Man, which will
be forgiven, and blaspheming against the Holy Spirit, which will never
be forgiven. Mark says simply: 'Let anyone blaspheme against the Holy
Spirit and he will never have forgiveness: he is guilty of an eternal sin,'
without establishing the distinction between blasphemy against the
Son of Man and blasphemy against the Spirit. Instead of the 'Son of
men', he talks of 'men', and as the subject of the malignant words, not
their object. Manson wonders what the original word was that has been
reproduced with more or less accuracy by each of the synoptics.[7] One
can, he claims, suppose an Aramaic original containing these three
elements: sins or malignant words, son of man, forgiveness. The tradition followed by Mark establishes the same connection: 'all men's sins
and all their blasphemies will be forgiven,' whereas the underlying
tradition of Q is: 'anyone who says a word against the Son of Man will
be forgiven.' But blasphemy against the Spirit, as Matthew calls him the
first time, or the Holy Spirit, as he calls him next, will never be forgiven.
Matthew, like Mark, places this statement in the context of the instruction given to the crowd in the course of the ministry in Galilee; Luke
puts it in a different context and a different place, in the perspective of
a situation which will lead the disciples to confess Jesus fearlessly and
in public – Lk. 12.11-12.

It seems likely that Mark has kept to the historical version of the
words of Jesus. Matthew uses these words instead of another sentence
from a different context, that of an exhortation addressed to the
disciples to prepare them for the moment when they will find themselves placed *in statu confessionis*. This exhortation occurs in all three
synoptics, but they place it at different moments, grouped in the
Synopsis of Benoit-Boismard in his para. 208, taking Lk. 12.1-12 as
the basis for the logic of the discourse. It is quite probable that Jesus
returned to the theme on several occasions, but above all, as in Mark's
presentation, during his last visit to Jerusalem. See Mt. 10.17-33; Mk.
8.38 and 13.9-13; Lk. 9.26; 21.12-18; 12.1-12, in which Luke distinctly
states: 'And he began to speak, first of all to his disciples.' Luke, who
wrote one book about the pre-pentecostal time of Jesus and his
disciples and another about their post-pentecostal time, re-introduces
into this pericope a statement that he himself (8.17) and the other
synoptics (Mt. 10.26; Mk. 4.22) report as belonging to another occasion: 'Everything that is now covered will be uncovered, and everything
now hidden will be made clear. What I say to you in the dark, tell in the
daylight . . .' This orientates our research into the meaning of the distinction made by Matthew and Luke between words against the Son of
Man and words against the Holy Spirit toward the difference of situation between the time of Jesus' earthly ministry on the one hand, and
the time of the Spirit given and operating with power in the words and

signs of the apostles on the other.

In Luke, it is not a question of the spirit (Spirit) through which *Jesus* cast out devils,[8] nor of the Son of Man, but of the Spirit. During Jesus's earthly ministry, *he* had the Spirit, but neither his disciples nor his audience did. So it was possible to misunderstand him. Christ showed himself in his weakness, so far from glory, so like other men . . . As St Jerome observes, 'He who scandalizes my flesh and strikes me as just a man, so that I follow the son of the carpenter, a glutton, a wine-drinker: such an appreciation, such a blasphemy, though based on culpable error, still has an excuse (*veniam*) by virtue of the baseness of the body'.[9] There were certainly some 'signs', but Jesus refused the demands of the Jews for a sign that was unequivocally from heaven (Mk. 8.11; Mt. 16.1; Jn. 6.30): there would be no sign other than that of Jonas, that is, preaching a call to conversion.[10] So that the time of Jesus' earthly ministry, the time of the non-glorious Son of Man — Lk. 12.8 and 10 imply a distinction between this and his glorious state — could have been a time of excusable ignorance. Luke insists particularly on this point. The supreme phrase, which he alone recounts, 'Father, forgive them, for they know not what they do' (23.24), is echoed in the words he puts into the mouth of Stephen: 'Lord, do not hold this sin against them' (Acts 7.60). Also in the words he attributes to Peter after the cure of a lame man in the Temple: 'neither you nor your leaders had any idea what you were really doing' (Acts 3.17: compare 13.27 *agnoèsantes*). If they had known the wisdom of God, says St Paul for his part, 'they would not have crucified the Lord of Glory' (1 Cor. 2.8); and again, speaking of himself: 'even though I used to be a blasphemer and did all I could to injure and discredit the faith. Mercy, however, was shown me, because until I became a believer I had been acting in ignorance' (1 Tim. 1.13 *agnoôn*).[11]

From that time onwards, we are no longer in the presence of Jesus in his mortal condition. The debate opened by his mission still remains open, but in different conditions. 'This Jesus whom you crucified, God has made Lord and Christ,' by raising him from the dead and glorifying him: Acts 2.16, 24; 3.15; 4.10; 5.30-32; 10.39-40; 13.30. Of this, Peter proclaims, we are the witnesses, we and the Holy Spirit (5.32; cf. Rom. 1.4). In effect, the whole of the Acts and of Paul's Epistles show the Spirit co-operating with the apostles, leading and strengthening their actions, concelebrating, in a way, with the witnesses to the Lord.[12] Jesus had promised: 'When the Advocate comes, whom I shall send to you from the Father, the Spirit of truth who issues from the Father, he will be my witness, and you too will be witnesses . . .' (Jn. 15.26-7; which corresponds to Lk. 24.48-9, and Acts 1.8).

The preaching of the apostles was accompanied, in both those who were sent out to preach and those who believed them, by a manifestation of the power of the Spirit: cf. Thess. 1.5-6, the earliest Christian text; 1 Cor. 2.4-5; 1 Pet. 1.12. Paul, who did not know Christ in the flesh, writes, 'Even if we did once know Christ in the flesh, that is not how we know him now (2 Cor. 5.16). Henceforth God's plan of salvation is openly unveiled and put into action, stemming from the resurrection and pentecost. To oppose it is to blaspheme against the Spirit.[13] It is to take up the closed, resistant attitude to God's work so often displayed by the Jewish people. The Isaiah of the exile reproached them for it: 'he proved himself their saviour in all their troubles . . . But they rebelled, they grieved his holy spirit' (63.8-10). And Stephen, himself filled with the Holy Spirit, repeats the rebuke: 'You stubborn people, with your pagan hearts and pagan ears. You are always resisting the Holy Spirit, just as your ancestors used to do' (Acts 7.51). They have the chance of being converted, as the apostles never cease to tell them. But a stubborn and basic opposition to the work of God places those who hold to it outside the eschatological gift of forgiveness of sins. The New Testament point of view, that of Luke in particular, is neither that of a theology of grace and penitence, nor that of the extent of the power of the keys, both of which have dominated the explanations of the Fathers and of theologians to an excessive extent. It is rather that of the particular conditions in which both the disciples and those who heard their preaching found themselves after Pentecost, the situation announced by the prophets as the messianic era, a pouring-out of the Spirit of holiness.[14]

This can clearly be seen when one looks for traces of this theme outside the synoptics. In the synoptics, Jesus is already announcing a time when the disciples will be called upon to confess him: Benoît-Besnard regroups the texts in the following way (para. 204), taking Lk. 12 as the guideline:

Mt. 10.26	= Mk. 4.22	= Lk. 8.17	= Lk. 12.2
Mt. 27-29			= Lk. 12.3-6
Mt. 10.30-32		= Lk. 21.18	= Lk. 12.7-8
Mt. 10.33	= Mk. 8.38	= Lk. 9.26	= Lk. 12.9
Mt. 12.32	= Mk. 3.29		= Lk. 12.10
Mt. 10.19-20	= Mk. 13.11	= Lk. 21.14-15	= Lk. 12.11-12

The disciples are seen as being *in statu confessionis*. Their witness bears on their faith in Jesus: he will deny before his Father those who have denied him before men — the reverse of Peter's confession in Mt. 16.16-19. The disciples are to be without fear or apprehension: the Spirit will show them what they must say. Luke sees no lack of logic in this sequence: 'I tell you, if anyone openly declares himself for me in the presence of men, the Son of Man will declare himself for him in the presence of God's angels. But the man who disowns me in the presence of men will be disowned in the presence of God's angels. Everyone who says a word against the Son of Man will be forgiven, but he who blasphemes against the Holy Spirit will not be forgiven' (12.8-10). What will be forgiven is the word against the Son of Man without the Holy Spirit, before the gift of the Spirit. But disowning the Son of Man once one has the assistance of the Spirit to recognize him and confess him merits being disowned by the Son of Man in heaven: compare 2 Tim. 2.12 and Apoc. 3.5. And, 'If anyone does not love the Lord, a curse on him' (1 Cor. 16.22); on the other hand, 'no one can be speaking under the influence of the Holy Spirit and say, "Curse Jesus", and no-one can say, "Jesus is Lord" unless he is under the influence of the Holy Spirit' (1 Cor. 12.3; cf. 1 Jn. 4.2-3; Eph. 1.17). It is worth noting that both Paul and John speak of 'Jesus' — he who came in his flesh, who appeared identical to men in his *kenosis* and who, exalted thereafter, is the object of the disciples' faith and witness: a host of texts state or imply this.[15] To betray this faith once one has received the gifts of the Spirit is to place oneself in the way of perdition. This is what the famous passages of the Epistle to the Hebrews and of the First Epistle of John state:

> *Heb. 6.4.* As for those people who were once brought into the light, and tasted the gift from heaven, and received a share of the Holy Spirit, *5.* and appreciated the good message of God and the powers of the world to come *6.* and yet in spite of this have fallen away — it is impossible for them to be renewed a second time. They cannot be repentant if they have wilfully crucified the Son of God and openly mocked him.
> *Heb. 10.26.* If, after we have been given knowledge of the truth, we should deliberately commit any sins, then there is no longer any sacrifice for them. *27.* There will be left only the dreadful prospect of judgment and of the raging fire that is to burn the rebels ... *29.* and you may be sure that anyone who tramples on the Son of God, and who treats the blood of the covenant which sanctified him as if it were not holy, and who insults the Spirit of grace, will be condemned to a far severer punishment ... *32.* Remember all the sufferings that you had to meet after you received the light, in earlier days ...

It is without doubt the sin apostasy, or more precisely the refusal to confess Jesus Christ come in the flesh[16] that John calls 'a sin that is death' (1 Jn. 5.16). Before becoming the sin of the disciples who by this fault were omitted from the prayer of the Church, this was previously the sin of the world for which Jesus did not pray (Jn. 17.9). But the Spirit has been sent to witness with the disciples (15.26-7), and before their consciousness, to the justice of Christ's cause, the sin of the world that has refused his light, and the overthrow of the devil.[17] He is the Paraclete, the advocate, the defender, who calls and consoles. The Apocalypse gives ample evidence of the persecution undergone by the disciples 'for witnessing to Jesus', but provides no particular text to illustrate our theme.

Neither Hebrews nor John speak of 'blasphemy'. The Apocalypse applies it to the Beast (13.1.5, 6) and the prostitute of Babylon (17.3). But there is no need for explicit words to be used to constitute blasphemy, as some commentators have argued: behaviour can be blasphemous or conducive to blasphemy.[18] H. W. Beyer has shown that raising oneself up against God's actions for the salvation of his people can constitute blasphemy (cf. 2 Kgs. 19.4, 6, 22), as can attributing God's saving grace and actions to another source: this is the accusation the Jews brought against Jesus.[19] From the Christian point of view, on the other hand, blasphemy consists in denying the attribution of messianic power and the quality of Lordship to Jesus, due to him as the one sent by the Father: during his earthly ministry, this involved attributing his power to cast out devils, which came from the Spirit he had been given, to Beelzebub; after pentecost, it meant refusing to recognize the action of the Spirit in the apostles and the life of the Church. This could apply either to the Jews, as in Acts 13.45, or to the Pagans. It could even apply to the disciples, placed *in statu confessionis* and persecuted, as Paul was obliged to remind them (Acts 26.11), and as the gospels, the epistles and even the Apocalypse foresee. This is why the Spirit is given to the disciples. To betray their witness to Jesus is to betray God's saving action, to blaspheme against the Spirit.[20]

One can add that heresy is often ascribed as blasphemous, since it amounts to denying the truth of God the Saviour: this is found in the Fathers, and as early as 2 Pet. 2.2.[21]

Translated by Paul Burns

Notes

1 *Sermo* 71.8 (PL 38.449).
2 J. Knabenbauer, 'De peccato in Spiritum Sanctum quod non remittetur', *Rev. Bib.* 1 (1892), pp. 161-170 — taken from his commentary on St Matthew in the famous *Cursus Scripturae Sacrae*.
3 Such as: E. Mangenot, 'Blasphème contre le Saint-Esprit', *Dict. Theol. cath.* II (1905), col. 910-6; H. Leisegang, *Pneuma Hagion* (Leipzig, 1922); A. Fridrichsen, 'Le péché contre le Saint-Esprit', *Rev. Hist. Philos. Relig.* 3 (1923), pp. 397-72; A. Michel, in *Ami du Clergé* (1924), p. 813; *ibid.* (1936), pp. 276-8; *ibid.* (1955), pp. 123-4; H. von Baer, 'Der Heilige Geist in den Lukasschriften', *Beitr. z. Wissensch. vom Alten u. Neuen Test.*, III, series H. 3 (Stuttgart, 1926); P. Roulin, 'Le Péché contre le Saint-Esprit', *Bible et vie Chrét.* 29 (Sept.-Oct. 1959), pp. 38-45; E. Lovestam, 'The Logion on Blasphemy against the Holy

Spirit', *Svensk Exeg. Årsb.* 33 (1968), pp. 101-117; *idem, Spiritus Blasphemia* (Lund, 1968); H. B. Swete, *The Holy Spirit in the New Testament* (London, 1909): though generally so valuable, he is somewhat disappointing on this subject.

4   Lev. 24.10-16; cf. 1 Kgs. 21.13; cf. Exod. 20.7; 22.27, whence Mk. 14.64; cf. Jn. 19.7.

5   The reason given by Bultmann is that this is contrary to the title 'Son of Man' found in Mt. and Lk.

6   Fridrichsen, *op. cit.*, p. 372. (1) If Jesus casts out devils by the same power as the Jews, how can he add, 'if it is through the Spirit of God that I cast devils out, then know that the kingdom of God has overtaken you'? (2) This does not explain the genesis of the Q version; F. Büchsel, *Der Heilige Geist im Neuen Testament* (Gutersloh, 1926), p. 179, n. 6; according to Leisegang, this stems from the view that *Pneuma* is tinged with Greek mysticism; von Baer, *op. cit.*, p. 142: there is not the least textual evidence for replacing 'Spirit' with 'name'. If Jesus had claimed to cast out devils in the name of God, one cannot see what the Scribes could have reproached him with.

7   W. Manson, 'The Gospel of Luke', *Moffatt's N. T. Comm.* (London, 1955), p. 152.

8   The sin encompassed by the term 'blasphemy' (attributing to Beelzebub what came from the Spirit) could already be unforgiveable if it stemmed from culpable hardening of the heart, from refusal to accept the evidence: and it was evident that he could not be casting out devils through the prince of devils . . .

9   *In Matt.*, PL 26.81. The allusions are to Mt. 19.55 (Lk. 3.23; Jn. 6.42); Mt. 11.19; 9.11; Lk. 15.1-2; 19.7. Knabenbauer quotes Chrysostom, Cyril of Alexandria, Bede, Paschase Radbert, Denys of Chartres, Cayetan, Jansen, Cornelius a Lapide, Calmet and various authors of the nineteenth century as voicing the same view. One can add O. Procksch, in *Theol. Wb. z. N. T.* I, p. 105; the Jerusalem Bible on Mt. 12.32; the Ecumenical version on Lk. 12.10.

10   Mt. 12.41; 16.4; Lk. 11.29-32 (Mt. 12.40 slants the sign of Jonas toward that of the resurrection). On the meaning of this text cf. E. Klosterman, *Das Matthäus-Evangelium* (1927), *in loc.*; W. G. Kümmel, *Verheissung und Erfüllung* (1953), pp. 61 ff.; A. Vogtle, *Der Spruch von Jonaszeichen* (1953), pp. 230-77; O. Glombitza, 'Das Zeichen des Jona zum Verständnis von Mt. 12.38-42', *N. T. Studies* 8 (1961-2), pp. 359-66; J. Howton, 'The Sign of Jonah', *Scott. Journ. of Theol.* 15 (1962), pp. 288-204.

11   The O. T. recognized the difference between faults committed inadvertently and those committed deliberately, and so deserving of death. Lev. 4.2 ff; 5.15; Num. 15.22-31. and v. H. von Baer, *op. cit.*, p. 141.

12   See 'Le Saint-Esprit et le Corps apostolique, réalisateurs de l'oeuvre du Christ', *Rev. Sc. philos. théol.* 36 (1952), pp. 613-25; 37 (1953), pp. 24-48.

13   According to E. Lövestam, *blasphemia Spiritus* = 'Opposition gegenüber Gott in seiner eschatologischen Heilstätigkeit', *op. cit., supra* n. 3, p. 62. Cf. H. W. Beyer, 'Blasphemia', *Theol. Wb. z. N. T.* I, pp. 620-4, on p. 623, 1.17 ff.: Mt. 12.32 should be taken as showing the conscious and impious rejection of God's power and grace, offered for man's salvation and healing. Only those who refuse the pardon are excluded from it. He quotes 1 Tim. 1.20: Paul hands men over to Satan to teach them not to be blasphemous.

14   Cf. Is. 11.2; 42.1; 61.1 ff.; (Lk. 4.18-19); Joel 3.1-5 (Acts 2.17-21). Cf. H. von Baer, *op. cit.*, p. 142.

15   V. e.g. Phil. 2.10-11; 1 Cor. 12.3; 1 Jn. 4.3; Acts 2.36; 3.6.

16   Cf. 1 Jn. 4.2-3: a version supported by Polycarp in *Ad Philipp.* 7.1.

17   Jn. 16.7-15. I am following the interpretation made by F. Berrouard and the authors he quotes: 'Le paraclet défenseur du Christ devant la conscience dur croyant', *Rev. Sc. philos. théol.* 33 (1949), pp. 361-389.

18   Cf. H. W. Beyer, *art. cit.*, p. 623, referring to 1 Tim. 6.1; Jn. 2.7; Rom. 2.24; Tit. 2-5.
19   Mk. 2.7 ff.; Jn. 10.33-6; Mk. 14.64 and Mt. 26.65.
20   A. Fridrichsen (cf. n. 3) has suggested an interpretation of Mt. and Lk. (Q source) distinguishing between the word against the Son of Man and blasphemy against the Spirit as the formula of a missionary maxim of the early Church, to distinguish between two categories of *lapsi*: those who simply denied Jesus and those who claimed that by abandoning themselves to the action of the *pneuma* they were in league with the devil.
21   H. W. Beyer, *art. cit.*, pp. 623-4, gives some representative references.

Langdon Gilkey

The Spirit and the Discovery
of Truth through Dialogue

AS the biblical and traditional sources of our faith make plain, the
Spirit is the activity of God within the Christian community and within
each believer enabling us to know the truth of the gospel and to embody that gospel in a new life. It is through God as the Spirit that God
is known; and it is through the love from God shed abroad in our
hearts that we love one another (Augustine). The Spirit is the inward
principle of the divine uniting with our own autonomous intellect
and will to remake us into knowers and doers of the truth; in Tillich's
felicitous language, the Spirit is the theonomous depth of our spirit in
all of the latter's creative functions. It is this 'doctrine' of the Spirit,
common to the classical traditions of Catholicism and Protestantism
alike, which I wish to discuss in relation to the new historical situation
in which we find ourselves. For implications of that new situation,
affirmed by us all, have in turn further implications for our conception
of the Spirit and of the ways it functions within the Christian community. These dual implications, as I shall seek to show, involve a new
conception of the Spirit as manifest in and through dialogue, dialogue
of the Church with culture on the one hand and dialogue within the
whole Church on the other. It is, needless to say, appropriate that this
theme of the Spirit as manifested in dialogue be addressed in an essay
presented in honour of Father Edward Schillebeeckx, O.P.; as much as
any contemporary Christian he has in his thought and his life coura-
geously embodied and creatively justified these new dialogical
implications concerning the work of the Spirit in the Church.

I. THE SPIRIT AND THE DIALOGUE WITH CULTURE

The new historical situation in which the Christian community, and so its theologians as well, finds itself has of course many facets. Central for our purpose is the new realization of the *historicity* of human being in its totality, and so the historicity of the thought and the action of men, women and so of their communities. By historicity in this sense I refer to the location of all thought and action within a cultural epoch; we think all our thoughts in terms of the cultural forms of our time, in terms, that is, of the self-interpretation of man and of his world which we share with the community of our time and place. As any contemporary understanding of the gospel — our present grasp of its truth — is inescapably within the particular forms of our experience and of our reflection on that experience, and so in relation to the science, the psychology, the social science, the literature, the arts and the philosophy expressive of the self-interpretation of our being in the world characteristic of our present cultural life. Contemporary Catholic theology, in its courageous attempt to come to grips with post-Kantian philosophy and to rethink many traditional theological symbols in these modern terms, illustrates this awareness of the inescapable interpenetration of theological reflection on our tradition with the reflective forms of self-interpretation characteristic of our epoch. Correspondingly, any praxis of the gospel, or theological interpretation of that praxis, is likewise set within the self-understanding of our cultural life, that is, in terms of its social and political understanding, and so on relation to critical social theory, economic and political understanding, as well as in terms of our modern interpretations of what authentic obligation entail and so our concepts of freedom, of responsibility and their relation to authentic community. The gospel is enacted by men and women *in* their social and historical situation, and thus is praxis reflectively interpreted by them in terms of the way they understand human being and its social world. Present Catholic ethics with its emphasis on social and political liberation manifests clearly this interpenetration of traditional themes of Christian ethics and Christian hope with contemporary social theory, with a new philosophy of human being and of human obligation as social in character, with a new interpretation of history and of temporal passage and their relation to social structures and social change. One could add as a final twist to our point that our theological consciousness of our historicity is *itself* an example of the effect of culture on theology since it was through the cultural developments of modernity that consciousness arose in the Christian community; and also the current *identity* of theological reflection and praxis is 'a gift from culture' stemming directly from Marxist and also from pragmatic and instrumentalist thought.

The first immediate consequence of this current awareness of the interpenetration of cultural forms with Christian symbols in both theological reflection and in praxis is that for none of us are theological or ethical understanding — Christian doctrine and Christian law — any longer absolute or autonomous, 'a se' and changeless above the shifting and relative forms of cultural history. As culture changes, so theology and Christian ethics change — and must, if they are to be meaningful, relevant and foundational for the people who live within that culture. The *relativity* of theological and ethical reflection to its cultural locus is the first implication of awareness of our historicity, and this poses the deeply painful question — felt by every present theologian and ethicist — of the relation of our relative theological truths and our relative ethical principles and laws to the divine truth and the divine norms to which both refer. Needless to say, this point forms the heart of the debate about both authority and infallibility in the Church: is there a *locus* in the Church, wherever it may be found, that is beyond cultural relativity, beyond change, and beyond criticism? Our point, therefore, goes to the heart of contemporary ecclesiastical issues as well as those concerning the status of doctrine, dogma and canon law.

The spectre of the ultimate relativity of our theological and ethical perspectives, as reflecting more of our cultural biases than they do of the divine truth and will, haunts all contemporary theology and ethics. If the Church speaks in theology and law with a cultural voice, how is the divine word to be heard among men and women? If all views are inescapably historical, can there be any relation to a divine and eternal truth? Clearly the sharpness and pain of these questions are reasons for the continuing strength of conservative forces present in all the churches, forces which seek to counter the spectre of relativism with the claim to possess an absolute truth and in inerrant guide to practice. The undeniable and so undenied fact of historicity raises thus a question of relativity within the Church's life — and calls for a reinterpretation of the Spirit as it relates to the historicity of human thinking.

The second implication of the historicity of all thought, and so of all religious thought, is that theology can only discover *its own* truth in explicit dialogue with its cultural setting. If we are historical, then we can only appropriate a truth in theology expressed in the reflective terms of our historicity, that is, in the thought-forms of our time, expressive of our self-interpretation and our interpretation of our world — but by the same token critical and transformative of that interpretation of self and world. Any other version of the truth of the gospel will be meaningless to us, uncritical and so untransformative of us — and anyway, we are all convinced that an 'uncultural' and so absolute statement of the gospel is in fact a cultural statement of that gospel from another time parading before our modern eyes as an eternal, changeless and so definitive statement. Present Catholic eschatological theology, expressed in terms of social reconstruction and liberation and set in an ontology of a moving historical continuum directed towards a new socio-historical future, illustrates this resetting of biblical eschatology in the terms of modern views of time, history, and social change, and thus is another example of the dialogical relation to cultural concepts in order to express to us a biblical and traditional symbol. If we be historical in our thought and life, the truth of the gospel can only be appropriated by and so transformative of us in dialogue with our cultural self-interpretation; out of that dialogue the divine message arises for us, is received by us and can be spoken through us.

This has always been so, as the Hellenic elements in the Patristic and medieval periods clearly show. But it is only in modernity that this has been clearly seen as an inescapable part of our finitude – and so an aspect of God's intention for us as finite creatures in time. If there be an answer to the question of the relativity that this dialogic character of theology and preaching necessarily implies, it must be found within a reinterpretation of the work of the Holy Spirit through whom the divine truth within the continuing moments of historical time is known. We may be sure that the Spirit is aware of the finitude and so the historicity of our minds – even the most faithful of minds – which God has given us as our creator. Thus we may be assured that the Spirit speaks its word *in* and *through* the dialogue between Church and culture out of which theological reflection arises. On no other basis may we have confidence in the traditions which we treasure as mediating to us the divine truth – *once* we have seen, as we all have, the relativity of the gospel as it was interpreted in those traditions to the cultural conditions in which those interpretations arose. The promise that the Spirit will always be with the community guiding it into the truth includes, therefore, the promise that it will illumine continually with the truth that community's life in all its historicity and so in all its cultural relativity. This is one meaning for the crucial phrase, foundational for all the certainty of Christian faith and theology: 'I believe in the Holy Spirit' as it illumines me in my present situation and as it illumines us in our common cultural situation. This is the only answer to the question of historical relativism; but it is, as with all of God's answers, a wholly sufficient one.

The Catholic Church has always been aware of the intrinsic relation of theological reflection to cultural wisdom here outlined, and in the light of that assurance it adopted Stoic, Platonic and Aristotelian philosophy and Stoic natural law theories as instruments for the expression of its gospel and its law. Interestingly enough, however, this dialogue with culture was made legitimate, if we may put it that way, through the symbol of the divine logos, known in part by all true philosophy and made flesh in the Christ. Thus as representing the same logos, philosophical and theological reflection were enabled to unite in the expression of the one divine truth. I too believe that participation in the logos, the rational structure and meaningfulness of reality as it unfolds, is essential to all knowing and shaping of our world, and thus that the use of this symbol is necessary to understand the legitimacy of the dialogue of faith and theology with culture. However, our new consciousness of the historicity of our cultural life and thought make the Spirit newly relevant as the mediating link, the principle of legitimacy, of our dialogue with culture. For we now understand that our thought — and the cultural life produced by that creative spirit — is not simply reproductive of a timeless objective structure; rather we know that it is also through the *creative* activity of the human spirit in its encounter with reality that a cultural 'world' is produced out of the creativity of its life. Thus in that sense we know that philosophy, social theory, anthropology and the sciences are less reflections of an eternal objective structure as themselves 'historical', productions of creative spirit — in dialogue, so to speak, with reality — through its language, its 'pre-ontological' structures and its norms, and its reflection on these, as these develop in time. The cultural worlds which philosophy unfolds and with which theology is in dialogue are products of the human spirit in its continuing yet varied historical encounters with reality. Thus if the dialogue between that aspect of our spiritual life which is enshrined in culture and that aspect of our spiritual life which interprets the gospel and which is enshrined in tradition and doctrine, is to be legitimated and secured, made secure against the threat of relativism and debilitating doubt, it must be in terms of the Spirit as the divine depth of *all* creative spiritual functions and so as the inward divine resource of truth, as well as in terms of the logos as the objective structure of reality's processes.

If, therefore, the Church correctly had once to recognize the universal presence of the logos in existence in order to legitimate its own self-understanding and theological construction as dialogue with philosophy, so too on the same grounds we must, in recognizing the historicity of both cultural and theological thought, affirm the universal work of the Spirit in human culture. The Spirit is at work in the world wherever truth is known and wherever community is formed, and so wherever men and women reach a coherent self-interpretation of themselves, their community and their world. Only on such a view can we give a *theological* ground for our assent to theological use of the natural, social and psychological sciences of psychology, philosophy and the arts in their appropriate realms. The whole trinity as the divine ground of our finite being, of finite logos, and of finite creative spirit is at work wherever there is existence, understanding and meaning — whenever there is a creative social order. The divine Spirit, dimly and partially reflected in cultural life, witnesses to and interpets for *its* time and Holy Spirit, the principle of truth and of community within the Church. Thus is our dialogue with culture rendered legitimate through the dual work of the Spirit. Above all thus is the relativity of *both* sides of the dialogue, inescapable for our finitude, rescued for faith by the participation of the same Spirit in cultural and in Church life alike. Wherever there is truth in cultural life, there the Spirit is at work; and where that truth is understood to illumine for us the meaning of the gospel in our existence, there the Spirit through our freedom brings to actuality in our present the Spirit that remains within the life of the community of faith. As in the early Church the criterion for the use of the universal logos was the logos made flesh, so for the Church now the criterion of the Spirit at work in the world is and must be the Spirit revealed in and through the originating symbols of the Church's life; the Spirit within the Church's life is the criterion of the Spirit at work in the world.

Needless to say, the same principles apply with increasing urgency to our dialogue with other religions whose spiritual power and whose truth, over against much that is dead in our own religious and Church life, is ever more apparent to us. We can enter into a constructive dialogue with them, recognizing the validity and power resident in them, with openness and yet with confidence because we know that the same Spirit that we know is at work in its own ways, often strange to us, in them. Otherwise we face them either with pride or with fear, neither one being a wise or a Christian attitude, and either one clearly inappropriate in our present situation.

Two further implications issue from this dialogic relation of theology to its cultural world, and the presence of the Spirit in both. (1) There can no longer be *even in principle* such a concept as the index, a list of cultural works excluded from the Christian consciousness. If theological interpretation in fact arises out of creative dialogue with culture, then it is fatal to theology as a reflective expression of faith — and so fatal to living faith — to close off the cultural voice from the Christian ear. And if the Spirit is at work, albeit hiddenly, in culture, then the Spirit's strange ways of judging, testing and refashioning Christian truth may be blocked by our lack of confidence in the unity of the Spirit. For if what we have said is true, we must study the strange and often 'offensive' voices of culture not only to combat or to convert them; we must study them in order to *learn* from them *and* to learn about our gospel from them. In this sense our own recent theological history establishes the latent or hidden presence of the

Spirit unquestionably in many of the most anti-clerical and even 'anti-Christian' voices of culture – as the logos was once said to be present in the pre-Christian and so 'pagan' philosophers. Is there any question that our present deeper understanding of our own gospel, in both theology and praxis, cannot possibly be conceived without themes provided for us by Spinoza, Voltaire and *die Aufklarung*, Marx, Nietzsche, Lyle and Darwin, Freud, Jung, Dewey, Heidegger and Bloch? – most of them hardly in their time regarded as enthusiastic churchmen! Now, however, they are (or should be) honoured by us as co-founders of much that is creative in our present theological understanding. If this is so, and it is, an index of books viewed at any given moment as antithetical to the faith by no means 'saves' the Church; in fact it threatens to exclude from our creative dialogue much of what the Spirit is strangely and hiddenly doing to refashion and so to redeem the Church.

(2) If all theological self-interpretation arises out of a serious dialogue with its cultural time and place, and only so can it arise, then there are *ipso facto* no definitive – universal, absolute and changeless – statements about faith and morals that are possible for the Church. Each Christian community, and each period of its life, inescapably – all our thought being historical and relative – reflects *one* perspective on the whole truth. Any definitive statement of the faith, therefore, has within it not only the 'crypto-heresy' that Father Rahner referred to; it also shares, in adopting as a part of itself the relativity of its culture, the relativity of all human thinking. The certainty of faith, that our commitment and understanding relate to something that transcends the relativity of all we think, will and do, is therefore not based on the absoluteness of our own theological, doctrinal and dogmatic statements; it is based on the confidence that the Spirit is present in the cultural forms we think with and in the view of the gospel we achieve with their help; and that through the consensus of the community concerning our theological interpretations the Spirit will manifest its truth for us and for our children as that truth comes to be out of the Spirit's work both in the world and in the Christian community. Despite our relativism – on both sides of the dialogue – we can trust in our relative truth – as Christians have always trusted – because of the promise of the presence of the Spirit in the world and in the Church. Perhaps it is through its strange work in modern culture generating the consciousness of the historicity of us all, that the Spirit has 'hiddenly' brought to *our* consciousness a better comprehension of the ways of the Spirit in the community of faith than that community had been able to achieve before!

II. THE SPIRIT AND THE DIALOGUE WITHIN THE CHURCH

If all our thought, experiencing and doing is *historical*, a perspective located in time and place on the world we encounter and on the self that encounters that world, then 'partiality' or 'incompleteness', that 'one-sidedness' endemic to our finitude and temporality, characterizes as well our various communal interpretations of the gospel. The way a particular communion embodies the faith in its existence, its piety, its practices and its understanding will be one perspective on the gospel, not the whole and entire truth of the gospel. This is evident to us all *historically* over the sequence of time. Patristic Christianity is, we know, a Hellenic-Roman embodiment of the faith, different in many important ways from the medieval embodiment and vividly different from the Catholic Church's seventeenth and eighteenth century forms — an understanding of change and relativity over time that is partly (but only partly) expressed in the phrase 'development of dogma'. The same — though this is more difficult to absorb — is true over space, in any given present, among the various communions: Orthodox, Roman Catholic, Anglican, the forms of Protestantism, each expressing historical and relative interpretations and perspectives on the infinite richness of the faith, each embodying the true Church in its own way, but in fragmentary, partial, historical form. None is a concrete absolute within the structure of time — as each form has tended to view itself before the advent of the consciousness of historicity. The alternative to this implication of our historicity is to regard these differences — and they are undeniable — not as stemming from differences of perspective on a mystery none fully embodies, but as one eternally right and several eternally wrong interpretations of the faith. But can any of us seriously say that Orthodoxy represents an eternally wrong interpretation of Christianity, a final embodiment of important error? This we all now find impossible to say — though Protestants and Roman Catholics alike have said it frequently enough in the past. Thus has the ecumenical movement arisen and grown, and thus do we all recognize other interpretations of the gospel as embodied in 'Churches' or forms of the one Church, rather than as sincere but errant 'religious associations'. Ecumenicity has grown as much out of the effect of our cultural consciousness of our historicity (derived, ironically, from the anti-clerical Enlightenment!) as it has out of a rebirth of Christian caritas among us or a renewal of biblical insight.

This partiality of perspective and so this incompleteness — despite the 'sufficiency' of each perspective through the divine grace — a Protestant realizes deeply in seeing the need on the part of *his* perspective on the gospel for the richness of the Catholic substance: for the sacramental presence of the divine, for the deep sense of tradition, for the experience and love of community, of being a 'people', and for the presence of caritas in the community — those elements of Catholic substance which every Protestant community desperately needs if it would be whole. And if I understand the creative, liberal movements within Catholicism aright, they represent an attempt on the part of the Catholic communion to incorporate into its like in genuinely *Catholic* form aspects of what has been called 'the Protestant principle' — an attempt more successful, I think, than corresponding efforts of Protestants to incorporate Catholic elements into their life. Communions within the whole Church, and divergent points of view within the differing communions, need one another for their wholeness. Once more dialogue — this time within the Church as a whole — is the way to the fullness of divine truth.

With historicity, moreover, the spectre of total relativism again seems to face us. If all communions, and all theological viewpoints within the various communions, are historically relative and religiously perspectival, how are we, how can we, be related at all to the divine truth which is by its very nature whole, one, universal and changeless? Does not the finitude and temporality of our every truth separate us inexorably from that which transcends time, space, and partiality? How can we be saved at all unless we embody the one whole divine truth in ourselves, in our institutions? Let us note that the rise of excessive dogmatism, not to say fanaticism, on the part of elements of each communion is more to be understood as an anxious reaction to the threat of relativism and so of total untruth than to the influence of rationalistic certitude; for one answer — and a poor, dangerous and ultimately futile answer it is — to the anxiety of relativism is to assert the absoluteness of one's own position. But, as we all deeply realize, the essence of the Christian faith is that we are saved by grace working in and through our finitude and our partiality, not by the absoluteness of our embodiment of the divine will and the divine truth. Thus conquest of our historicity comes — as *all* Christian salvation comes — through the divine promise of the Spirit to be present in our midst redeeming, recreating and completing our finite and fragmentary perspectives. In a quite new way we can see that the Church, now understood as *historical*, is utterly dependent on that promise and cannot at all be the Church without it. The meaning of that promise, crucial for the Church, is not that the perspective and the truth that any communion possesses is absolute, but precisely the opposite: that within the finitude, the partiality and the relativity of what we are, the Spirit is at work relating us to the divine truth we all seek and seek to embody.

If on the *divine* side — and the Church is always a divine human institution, a continuation in a strange way of the incarnation — it is the promise of the Spirit within our fragmentary perspectives that relate us to the wholeness of truth, on the *human* side that relation is achieved through the reality of our dialogue with one another. Where all expressions of truth are *historical*, fragmentary and partial, creative relation to the truth is achieved only by dialogue, by the encounter of one partial position with the criticism and the supplementation of another, rather than by the isolation and frozen perpetuation of one fragmentary perspective. Again a Protestant realizes this well: Protestant partiality becomes Protestant error if it fails to complement and to supplement its perspective with the polar reality of Catholic witness. Correspondingly one theological position exchanges its merely finite one-sidedness for serious error if it does not welcome the balance, judgment and refinement it receives from opposing viewpoints. Among historical beings truth appears in dialogue, arising dialectically out of the confrontation of opposites, and the new and richer consensus that may appear in the Spirit out of that confrontation – and in no other way.

The immediate implication of this truth of our historical finitude and of the working of the Holy Spirit among us – the new meaning of the old promise on which the Church is founded – is that the essential condition for truth within the community is the freedom of theological debate and so, paradoxically, the apparent tolerance of error. To stifle debate is not to preserve the whole truth – if *all* viewpoints be historical – but only to preserve the one-sidedness, fragmentariness and relativity of the truth we have. It is to transform relative truth into frozen error. The creative role of deviance in the history of doctrine is undoubted; the achievement of orthodoxy at every stage is historically inconceivable without the debate among deviant positions that preceded that achievement. But by the same token, 'orthodoxy' represents a *historical* consensus to be further balanced, criticized and refined by subsequent debate as cultural situations shift, interpretations of the gospel change, and as the relativity of even that consensus becomes plain. Only in the dynamic working of the Holy Spirit through the various perspectives of the whole Church is orthodoxy 'orthodox' – not in the absoluteness of one perspective within the whole.

Furthermore, this free and open elaboration of divergent points of view – essential for theological truth – must include debate on every level of doctrine, foundations as well as periphery, fundamental doctrines as well as subsidiary ones, ecclesiology and Christology as well as issues of method or of faith and reason. Otherwise partiality and anachronism become the hidden authorities at the *base* of our interpretation, and the crypto-heresy intrinsic to every particular foundation infects, because it is uncriticized and so untransformed, all the other aspects of theological work. If the Spirit works through all our thinking

67

and so all our theological interpretations, then the only way it can work *through* that historicity is by means of an unrestricted and foundational dialogue in which divergent positions are openly presented and freely debated. Through that dialogic encounter within the whole community, and only through that, can the partiality of each be judged and re-fashioned, and a larger truth achieved.

This understanding of the mode of relation to the truth of historical beings is, interestingly, itself an example of a gift to the Church of the Spirit as it worked 'hiddenly' in culture; for this understanding of truth as approximation rather than possession, and an approximation that grows through criticism and debate, is an interpretation of the truth that the scientific community has given to us all. It is, however, also intrinsic − though far too long obscured − to a religion based on grace and the Spirit: it is never what we possess, express or embody, whether in faith or in works, that is the basis of our confidence, the principle of the conquest of our finitude and our sin; rather it is the divine activity in and through our partiality and waywardness which is the ground of our confidence and certainty. This is as true of our community's relation to the truth as it is of our personal existence. Our historicity as our sin is redeemed and completed by the presence of the Spirit working within our divergences and their encounters to maintain the truth among us, and in that way, as it is promised to us, will the Spirit be with us to the end of the world. Partiality of viewpoint and freedom of debate do not, as conservative Catholics and Protestants alike feel, so much deny the presence of the Spirit as call for it and embody its activity. And they do not dispense with the need for authority within the Church community so much as give it a new and creative role: the role of expressing the consensus of the community as a theological discussion reaches its term *so that* out of a *new* and *open* debate new interpretations moving beyond that consensus may be embarked upon in the Spirit.

Bernard Lonergan

Mission and the Spirit

AS man's being is being-in-the-world, his self-understanding has to be not only of himself but also of his world. So biblical writers not only employed Babylonian cosmology but also re-interpreted it. In similar vein Arabic philosophers remodelled Ptolemy's heavens, and in turn Aquinas reformulated their views on the order of the universe. Today with evolution naming the shape of things, Karl Rahner has written on 'Christology within an Evolutionary View of the World'.[1]

Rahner prudently omitted from his account the long series of discontinuities reaching from subatomic particles to mankind. But the omission only makes the more prominent the greatest discontinuity of all, the transition from the natural to the supernatural. Indeed, for Rahner this transition is especially arduous, for he is committed to the anthropological turn and, on that view, nature gives way to spirit, the supernatural at its root is divine self-communication in love, and the obedient potency of a formal ontology has to be translated into terms of consciousness.

I have been using Rahner to state the question I wish to discuss. It reads: What in terms of human consciousness is the transition from the natural to the supernatural? With that question alone am I at present concerned. No doubt, related questions abound. But in this paper I beg to leave them in abeyance.

I. VERTICAL FINALITY

By 'finality' I would name not the end itself but relation to the end, and I would distinguish absolute finality, horizontal finality, and vertical finality.

Absolute finality is to God. For every end is an instance of the good, and every instance of the good has its ground and goal in absolute goodness.

Horizontal finality is to the proportionate end, the end that results from what a thing is, what follows from it, and what it may exact.

Vertical finality is to an end higher than the proportionate end. It supposes a hierarchy of entities and ends. It supposes a subordination of the lower to the higher. Such subordination may be merely instrumental, or participative, or both, inasmuch as the lower merely serves the higher, or enters into its being and functioning, or under one aspect serves and under another participates.[2]

The classicist view of the universe acknowledges hierarchy and the instrumental type of vertical finality. An evolutionary view adds 'he participative type: subatomic particles somehow enter into the elements of the periodic table; chemical elements enter into chemical compounds, compounds into cells, cells in myriad combinations and configurations into the constitution of plant and animal life.

Still one does not reach the evolutionary view simply by acknowledging hierarchy and the instrumental and participative types of vertical finality. An evolutionary view is a view of the universe. It can be fully grasped only by attending to the cause of the universe. For it is only as an instrument operating beyond its own proportion that the lower, as long as it is lower, can bring about and participate in the constitution of the higher; and it is only the cause of the whole universe that from lower species can bring about the emergence of successive higher species.

II. PROBABILITY AND PROVIDENCE

A theologian, if he thinks of evolution, turns to divine providence. A contemporary scientist that does so thinks of probabilities. Darwin's accumulations of chance variations have gained respectibility as probabilities of emergence. His survival of the fittest becomes probabilities of survival. What holds for living things, also holds in inanimate nature. Quantum theory has ended the long reign of mechanist determinism and has enthroned statistical law.

An evolutionary view of the universe, at a first approximation, would be a conditioned sequence of assemblies. Each assembly would be an environment with its constituent species. It would function on the basis of classical law, and consequently it would continue to function until the disruption of its interdependent factors resulted from internal deterioration or external interference.

From any assembly to the next there would be a cumulative

sequence of elements, where each element had its probability of emergence from the probability of survival of previously realized assemblies and elements.

In some such fashion, from a minimal beginning, schedules of probabilities of elements would link the emergence of successive assemblies of interdependent and mutually supporting factors. Granted very large numbers and very long intervals of time, Bernoulli's theorem of large numbers or, better, the De Moivre-Laplace limit theorem would make all but certain some close approximation to each step in the process.

When men operate on the small scale and can take all eventualities into account, they plan. When relevant factors are too numerous, combinations of agents too complicated, sufficiently accurate enumerations and measurements too difficult, then they have recourse to statistical science. But the omniscient and omnipotent cause of the whole universe does not operate blindly. He plans where men turn to probabilities. Nor does there come into existence, outside his planning, any agent that could interfere with his comprehensive design.[3]

III. THE SUPERNATURAL

Contemporary English usage commonly associates the supernatural with the spooky. But the term has a far older meaning, to which we have already adverted in speaking of vertical finality. For in a hierarchy of beings, any higher order is beyond the proportion of lower orders and so is relatively supernatural to them. But the infinite absolutely transcends the finite. It follows that the divine order is beyond the proportion of any possible creature and so is absolutely supernatural.

Our inquiry is with the absolutely supernatural. It regards man's vertical finality to God. It regards such vertical finality in the strictest sense, so that man is not merely subordinate to God but also somehow enters into the divine life and participates in it. When Rahner writes on Christology within an evolutionary perspective, he very explicitly means that there is a threefold personal self-communication of divinity to humanity, first, when in Christ the Word becomes flesh, secondly, whn through Christ men become temples of the Spirit and adoptive sons of the Father, thirdly, when in a final consummation the blessed know the Father as they are known by him.

This threefold personal self-communication of divinity is the end. On this end much has been written. It need not be recalled here, for our concern is not with the end but with finality to it, with that finality as evolutionary, with that evolutionary finality as it enters into human consciousness.

Vertical finality is to its end, not as inevitable, but as a possibility.

Its ends can be attained. They need not be attained. They may or may not be attained.

Vertical finality is multivalent. There need not be just one end beyond a given proper proportion. Indeed, the lower a being is in a hierarchic scale, the more numerous are the higher ends beyond its proper reach.

Vertical finality is obscure. When it has been realized in full, it can be known. When it is in process, what has been attained can be known, but what has not, remains obscure. When the process has not yet begun, obscurity prevails and questions abound. Is it somehow intimated? Is the intimation fleeting? Does it touch our deepest aspirations? Might it awaken such striving and groaning as would announce a new and higher birth?

Vertical finality to God himself is not merely obscure but shrouded in mystery. In this life we can know God, not as he is in himself, but only by deficient analogy. God himself remains mystery. Since potency is known by its act, relation by its term, it follows that vertical finality to God himself can be known only in the measure that God is known, that it can be revealed only in the measure that God himself has been revealed, that it can be intimated perhaps but hardly in a manner that is unambiguous since vertical finality is multivalent and obscure, and intimations are not apt to make clear which of many possibilities lies in store.

Vertical finality enters into evolutionary perspective. It does so inasmuch as emergence, unfolding, development, maturity follow the analogy of evolutionary process. Such process is to be understood in accord with emergent probabilities and under divine planning and action. By the analogy of that process is meant, not some basis for *a priori* prediction, but only a basis for *a posteriori* interpretation. Here as elsewhere, things are known in so far as they are in act.

IV. THE HUMAN SUBJECT

In a celebrated passage Aristotle granted that his ideal of the theoretic life was too high for man and that, if one lived it, one would do so not as a man but as having something divine present within one. None the less he went on to urge us to dismiss those that would have us resign ourselves to our mortal lot. He pressed us to strive to the utmost to make ourselves immortal and to live out what was finest in us. For that finest, though slight in bulk, still surpassed by far all else in power and in value.[4]

It is not hard to discern in this passage an acknowledgement of vertical finality in its multivalence and in its obscurity. In its multivalence, for there is in man a finest; it surpasses all else in power and in value; it is to be let go all the way. In its obscurity, for what is the divine in man, and what would be going all the way?

One has only to shift, however, from the corpus of Aristotelian writings to that of the Christian tradition, to recognize in Aristotle's position a sign of things to come. So Christian humanists have spoken of a *praeparatio evangelica* in the gentile world and, more bluntly, St Paul said to the Athenians: 'What you worship but do not know — that is what I now proclaim' (Acts 17.23).

If in the Greek patristic tradition *theoria* became the name of contemplative prayer, if medieval theolgians derived from Aristotle's principles an argument that man naturally desired to know God by his essence, it still remains that Aristotle's thought offered rather stony ground for the objectification of the life of the spirit. For the priority accorded the object gave metaphysics a dominant role. Psychology had to think in terms of potencies, or faculties, that were not among the data of consciousness. Worse, since psychology envisaged plant as well as animal and human life, the relation of operation to object was conceived, not precisely as intentionality, but vaguely as causality.[5] Further, the priority of objects entailed a priority of intellect over will, since will was conceived as rational appetite; and on the priority of intellect over will, there somehow followed a priority of speculative over practical intellect.

Intentionality analysis yields a contrasting picture of the subject. Along with the rest of modern science, it eschews dependence on metaphysics. For metaphysicians do not agree. A critically constructed metaphysics presupposes a theory of objectivity, an epistemology. An epistemology has to distinguish between knowing, as illustrated by any cognitional operation, and adult human knowing, which is constituted by a set of cognitional operations that satisfy a normative pattern. It follows that the single cognitional operation is neither a merely immanent psychological event nor yet a properly objective cognitional attainment. It has the intermediate status of an intentional act: as given, it refers to some other; but the precise nature and validity of that reference remains to be determined; and such determination is reached through the further intentional operations needed to complete the pattern constitutive of full objectivity. In a word, phenomenology brackets reality to study acts in their intentionality. In the very measure that it prescinds from questions of objectivity, it all the more efficaciously prepares the way for a convincing epistemology.

Intentionality analysis, like the rest of modern science, begins from the given. Unlike the rest of modern science, which dilates upon electrons and viruses, it can remain with the given, with human intentional operations dynamically related in their self-assembling pattern.

In its broad lines this dynamism rests on operators that promote activity from one level to the next. The operators are *a priori*, and they alone are *a priori*. Their content is ever an anticipation of the next level of operations and thereby is not to be found in the contents of the previous level.

Such operators are questions for intelligence: with respect to data they ask why, and what, and what for, and how, and how often. Such also are questions for reflection: with respect to the guesses, inventions, discoveries of human understanding they ask: Is that so? Are you sure? Such thirdly are questions for deliberation: they ask whether suggested courses of action are feasible, worth while, truly good or only apparently good.

Three types of operator yield four levels of operation. Each lower level is an instance of vertical finality, and that finality is already realized as the higher levels function. The lower level, accordingly, prepares for the higher and sublated by it.

We experience to have the materials for understanding; and understanding, so far from cramping experience, organizes it, enlarges its range, refines its content, and directs it to a higher goal. We understand and formulate to be able to judge, but judgment calls for ever fuller experience and better understanding; and that demand has us clarifying and expanding and applying our distinctions between astronomy and astrology, chemistry and alchemy, history and legend, philosophy and myth, fact and fiction. We experience and understand and judge to become moral: to become moral practically, for our decisions affect things; to become moral interpersonally, for our decisions affect other persons; to become moral existentially, for by our decisions we constitute what we are to be.

Such vertical finality is another name for self-transcendence. By experience we attend to the other; by understanding we gradually construct our world; by judgment we discern its independence of ourselves; by deliberate and responsible freedom we move beyond merely self-regarding norms and make ourselves moral beings.

The disinterestedness of morality is fully compatible with the passionateness of being. For that passionateness has a dimension of its own: it underpins and accompanies and reaches beyond the subject as experientially, intelligently, rationally, morally conscious.

Its underpinning is the quasi-operator that presides over the transition from the neural to the psychic. It ushers into consciousness not only the demands of unconscious vitality but also the exigences of vertical finality. It obtrudes deficiency needs. In the self-actualizing subject[6] it shapes the images that release insight; it recalls evidence that is being overlooked; it may embarrass wakefulness, as it disturbs sleep, with the spectre, the shock, the shame of misdeeds. As it channels into consciousness the feedback of our aberrations and our

74

unfulfilled strivings, so for the Jungians it manifests its archetypes through symbols to preside over the genesis of the ego and to guide the individuation process from the ego to the self.[7]

As it underpins, so too it accompanies the subject's conscious and intentional operations. There it is the mass and momentum of our lives, the colour and tone and power of feeling, that fleshes out and gives substance to what otherwise would be no more than a Shakespearian 'pale cast of thought'.

As it underpins and accompanies, so too it overarches conscious intentionality. There it is the topmost quasi-operator that by intersubjectivity prepares, by solidarity entices, by falling in love establishes us as members of community. Within each individual vertical finality heads for self-transcendence. In an aggregate of self-transcending individuals there is the significant coincidental manifold in which can emerge a new creation. Possibility yields to fact and fact bears witness to its originality and power in the fidelity that makes families, in the loyalty that makes peoples, in the faith that makes religions.

But here we meet the ambiguity of man's vertical finality. It is natural to man to love with the domestic love that unites parents with each other and with their children, with the civil love that can face death for the sake of one's fellow men, with the all-embracing love that loves God above all.[8] But in fact man lives under the reign of sin, and his redemption lies not in what is possible to nature but in what is effected by the grace of Christ.

Before advancing to that high theme, let us remark that an intentionality analysis can provide an apt vehicle for the self-objectification of the human subject. Let us note too that the old questions of priority, of intellectualism and voluntarism and the like, are removed and in their stead comes what at once is simple and clear. Lower levels of operation are prior as presupposed by the higher, as preparing materials for them, as providing them with an underfooting and, in that sense, with foundations. But the higher have a priority of their own. They sublate the lower, preserving them indeed in their proper perfection and significance, but also using them, endowing them with a new and fuller and higher significance, and so promoting them to ends beyond their proper scope.

Further, when so understood, priorities lose their rigidities. One might accord metaphysical necessity to such adages as *ignoti nulla cupido* and *nihil amatum nisi praecognitum*. But while they assert the priority of knowledge as one ascends from the lower to the higher, they tend to overlook the inverse priority by which the higher sublates the lower. It is in the latter fashion that orthopraxy has a value beyond orthodoxy. And surely the priority of the lower sets no rule that God must observe when he floods our inmost hearts with his love through the Holy Spirit he has given us (Rom. 5.5).

V. MISSION OF THE SON AND GIFT OF THE SPIRIT

The divine secret, kept in silence for long ages but now disclosed (Rom. 16.25), has been conceived as the self-communication of divinity in love. It resides in the sending of the Son, in the gift of the Spirit, in the hope of being united with the Father. Our question has been how to apprehend this economy of grace and salvation in an evolutionary perspective and, more precisely, how it enters into the consciousness of man.

First, I think, there is an awareness of a need for redemption. Human progress is a fact. There is a wheel that, as it turns, moves forward. Situations give rise to insights; insights into new courses of action; new courses of action to changed situations; changed situations to still further insights, further action, further change in situations. But such progress is only a first approximation to fact, for it is marred and distorted by sin. There is the egoism of individuals, the securer egoism of groups, the over-confident short-sightedness of common sense. So the intelligence of progress is twisted into the objectification of irrational bias. Worse, to simple-minded sins of greed there is added the higher organization of sophistry. One must attend to the facts. One must deal with them as in fact they are and, as they are irrational, obviously the mere dictates of reason are never going to work. So rationalization enters the inner citadel. There is opened a gap between the essential freedom all men have and the effective freedom that in fact they exercise. Impotent in his situation and impotent in his soul, man needs and may seek redemption, deliverance, salvation. But when it comes, it comes as the charity that dissolves the hostility and the divisions of past injustice and present hatred; it comes as the hope that withstands psychological, economic, political, social, cultural determinisms; it comes with the faith that can liberate reason from the rationalizations that blinded it.[9]

Secondly, the new order (2 Cor. 5.17) comes in the visible mission of the Son. In him is presented: (1) the absolutely supernatural object, for he is God; (2) the object for us, for he is man; (3) for us as to be redeemed, for he dies to rise again. As visible, he is the sacrament of man's encounter with God. As dying and rising, he shows the way to the new creation. As himself God, already he is Emmanuel, God with us.

Thirdly, besides the visible mission of the Son there is the invisible mission of the Spirit. Besides *fides ex auditu*, there is *fides ex infusione*.[10] *The former mounts up the* successive levels of experiencing, understanding, judging, deliberating. The latter descends from the gift of God's love through religious conversion to moral, and through religious and moral to intellectual conversion.[11]

These three are cumulative. Revulsion from the objective reign of sin and from the subject's own moral impotence heightens vertical finality. Without the visible mission of the Word, the gift of the Spirit is a being-in-love without a proper object; it remains simply an orientation to mystery that awaits its interpretation. Without the invisible mission of the Spirit, the Word enters into his own, but his own receive him not.

Such Christian origins are exemplary. As the Father sent the Son, so the Son sent the disciples on a mission to continue to the end of time. As the Father and the Son sent the Spirit to the disciples, so they continue to bestow the Spirit on the ever oncoming members of Christ. So the self-communication of the Son and the Spirit proceeds through history by a communication that at once is cognitive, constitutive, and redemptive: it is cognitive, for it discloses in whom we are to believe; it is constitutive, for its crystallizes the inner gift of the love of God into overt Christian fellowship; it is redemptive, for it liberates human liberty from thraldom to sin, and it guides those it liberates to the kingdom of the Father.

Experience of grace, then, is as large as the Christian experience of life. It is experience of man's capacity for self-transcendence, of his unrestricted openness to the intelligible, the true, the good. It is experience of a twofold frustration of that capacity: the objective frustration of life in a world distorted by sin; the subjective frustration of one's incapacity to break with one's own evil ways. It is experience of a transformation one did not bring about but rather underwent, as divine providence let evil take its course and vertical finality be heightened, as it let one's circumstances shift, one's dispositions change, new encounters occur, and — so gently and quietly — one's heart be touched. It is the experience of a new community, in which faith and hope and charity dissolve rationalizations, break determinisms, and reconcile the estranged and the alienated, and there is reaped the harvest of the Spirit that is '. . . love, joy, peace, patience, kindness, goodness, fidelity, gentleness, and self-control' (Gal. 5.22).

Notes

1   Karl Rahner, *Theological Investigations* (London and Baltimore, 1966), V, pp. 157-192.

2   On vertical finality see my papers 'Finality, Love and Marriage' and 'The Natural Desire to See God', *Collection, Papers by Bernard Lonergan*, ed. F. E. Crowe (New York and London, 1967), pp. 16-53 and 84-95.

3   On statistical inquiry, B. Lonergan, *Insight* (London and New York, 1957), pp. 53 ff.; on emergent probability, *ibid.*, pp. 121 ff., 259 ff. On Aristotle and Aquinas on world order, B. Lonergan, *Grace and Freedom, Operative Grace in*

the Thought of St. Thomas Aquinas, ed. J. Patout Burns (London and New York, 1971), ch. 4. One the origins of the notion of the supernatural, *ibid.*, pp. 13-19.

4   Aristotle, *Eth. Nic.*, X, 7, 1177b 26 and 32.

5   Aquinas, *In II de Anima*, lect. 6 #305 (Marietti).

6   On deficiency and growth motivation, Abraham Maslow, *Towards a Psychology of Being* (Princeton, 1962), ch. 3.

7   Erich Neumann, *The Origins and History of Consciousness* (Princeton, 1970) (original German edition: *Ursprungsgeschichte des Bewusstseins* [Zürich, 1949]). Gerhard Adler, *The Living Symbol, A Case Study in the Process of Individuation*, Bollingen Series LXII (New York, 1961).

8   Aquinas holds that apart from corrupt nature man naturally loves God above all: *Sum. theol.*, I-II, q. 109, a. 3 c. and as 1m.

9   This paragraph summarizes what I wrote in *Insight*, pp. 214-242, 619-633, 688-703, 718-730.

10   *Sum. theol.*, II-II, q. 6, a. 1.

11   B. Lonergan, *Method in Theology* (London and New York, 1972), pp. 122, 243.

Hans Küng

Confirmation as the Completion of Baptism

THIS article is intended as an approach to one of the most difficult themes of sacramental theology, to which Edward Schillebeeckx has contributed a large part of his written work.[1] In this short article, however, I can only formulate and explicate a few theses which might well seem far too attenuated to those who are acquainted with the complex network of exegetical, historical, systematic and practical problems of the subject. Nevertheless my remarks here comprise a summary of what I have said in various lectures.[2] An extended demonstration of the basis of my argument will follow, both in the form of a monograph on confirmation[3] and within a comprehensive doctrinal treatment of the sacraments.[4]

I. IS CONFIRMATION A SEPARATE SACRAMENT?

Theological uncertainty regarding the sacrament of confirmation has been considerable for some time. Its origins are mysterious; the rite has been subject to change, and the significance attributed to it contradictory. The various problems are comprised in the big question: Is it really possible to distinguish from baptism, which already mediates the Holy Spirit, yet another independent sacrament of bestowal of the Spirit? In this regard, indeed, confirmation seems to lack all the important characteristics: institution by Christ, a constant external sign, a special effect alongside that of baptism, necessity for salvation. The minister and his power, the recipient and his age are all questionable. This uncertainty cannot be resolved without recourse to origins and tradition, apart from which even today a new theological definition and practical reform are subject to purely arbitrary treatment and therefore vacillation.

1. A Special Sacrament in the New Testament?

(a) In the entire New Testament there is no text, word or sign of Jesus's which reports any institution of confirmation by him. On the other hand, there would seem to be indirect references in the New Testament which allow one to infer such an event.

(b) Throughout the New Testament, and especially in Paul and John, the bestowal of the Spirit is associated with *baptism*.

(c) That also applies to Luke and his Acts (cf. 1.5; 2.38; 9.17 ff.; 11.16): The account of Pentecost, presented as a baptism in the Spirit for the apostles, connects the bestowal of the Spirit as far as the faithful are concerned with baptism, and there is no question of any laying on of hands, let alone of confirmation. Hence those who have characterized Pentecost as the 'first confirmation' are wrong.

(d) In relation to this general finding, two texts in Acts which some would use as the basis for an independent sacrament of confirmation seem to be *exceptions* whose very irregularity indicates the *connection* between baptism and the reception of the Spirit. Both according to the account of the laying on of hands by the apostles in Samaria (8.14-7) and that of John's disciples in Ephesus (19.1-7), a baptism which does not bestow the Spirit is not essentially an authentic baptism, but has to be supplemented by reception of the Spirit (according to the story of the centurion Cornelius and the reception of the Spirit by the gentiles [Acts 10.44-8], the bestowal of the Spirit by God signifies on the other hand that baptism may not be refused to those who have received the grace of God: the bestowal of the Spirit and baptism belong together).

(e) Both these exceptional texts, whose historical imprecision and contradictions are made much of by the commentators, can be understood only in terms of their purpose and of the overall theological conception of the Lukan Acts (cf. Käsemann, Conzelmann, Haenchen). In the interests of the Church as threatened by gnosticism and heretics, and of the continuity of salvation history, Luke obviously adapted the original stories so that they could be inserted in his theologically determined account of the history of the primitive community:

i. The disciples of John (who in fact knew nothing of the preliminary nature of the Baptist and of the Spirit) became a special kind of Christian ('disciples', 'believers'): they (inconceivably) know nothing of the Spirit and are received into the apostolic Church by the laying on of hands, so that they no longer appear as competitors of Jesus's disciples (as with the transformation of the Apollos story in Acts 18.24-8).

ii. The relatively autonomous church of Samaria, which was actually missionized by Philip without any express commission, is said to have been received into communion with the apostolic Church by the apostolic visitation, and into communion with Jerusalem as its centre of unity. Only then, according to Luke, was the Spirit entrusted to it (the Cornelius story is similar in theological terms, for there the mission to the gentiles is subsequently ascribed to the will of God by the preceding bestowal of the Spirit).

(f) Hence these texts are directed to the integration of ecclesiastical outsiders in Samaria and Ephesus into the one Church under the supremacy of Jerusalem and the circle of the Twelve. Their central theme is not the notion of baptism but that of the Church, seen against the background of a salvation history orientated from an Old Testament basis at Jerusalem and emanating from Jerusalem at the midpoint of time.

(g) Both these theologically comprehensible yet historically questionable texts make a separation of baptism and the bestowal of the Spirit seem illegitimate from the start. In view of the unmistakable New Testament witness regarding the unity of baptism and the conferring of the Spirit, they offer no basis for a separate sacrament of the reception of the Spirit. They were not understood thus in the early history of the Church.

2. A Sacrament Apart in Ancient Church Tradition?

(a) On the basis of the New Testament evidence, is it perhaps possible to explain the complete silence of the sources in regard to a separate sacrament of the bestowal of the Spirit in the immediate period thereafter? *Second century* tradition knows nothing of an institution by Christ and nothing of a special sacrament of confirmation. In strict continuity with the New Testament itself in this period, baptism by water and baptism by water alone is the sacrament of reception of the Spirit. The 'seal of the Spirit' is imparted not by a laying on of hands after baptism — of which we have no witnesses in this century — but by immersion in water.

(b) Only in the *third century* — mainly in Tertullian and Hippolytus — (and in connection with baptism) do rites occur from which the total structure of the rite of confirmation later emerged: the laying on of hands, anointing, signing with the cross, and in Rome a special, second post-baptismal anointing of unknown provenance which was highly significant for the development of the later rite of confirmation. Yet it is a *petitio principii* to argue the existence of a specific sacrament from the mere existence of such rites.

(c) Neither Tertullian nor Hippolytus refers to the laying on of hands mentioned in Acts. Cyprian is the first to do that. He nevertheless represents baptism with water as imparting the Spirit in his fulness.

For Cyprian there is no difference between 'baptized' and 'confirmed'. Apart from this laying on of hands by which the Spirit is imparted, as described by Cyprian there is no evidence whatsoever in the third century that anointing, laying on of hands and signing, either separately or as a whole, ensured a post-baptismal bestowal of the Spirit. Even the word 'confirmation' was not used in this context before the third century.

(d) Even in *later patristic times*, despite the development of post-baptismal rites (insofar as they existed) the Spirit was still given in baptism. The post-baptismal rites were carried out together with baptism, and do not bestow any special gift of specific sacramental effect. That is also true for Ambrosius, who used the word 'confirmation' at this time; or for Jerome, who already marked episcopal visita- tions with the laying on of hands; or for Augustine, who was responsible for the emphasis on the doctrine of original sin and there-fore the baptism of infants. The post-baptismal rites remain an integral part of baptism as the one and only sacrament of initiation. The theology of initiation remains essentially a theology of baptism.

(e) It is quite understandable why the *Eastern Churches* have until today had no separate rite of confirmation (and only a post-baptismal anointing directly connected with baptism), and consequently (apart from later accommodations to western developments) no special theology of confirmation. The East keeps to the old tradition: the presbyter administers baptism together with the post-baptismal rites.

3. The Origin of the Western Rite of Confirmation

(a) Only in the Latin West was there the special development of a separation (in time and place) of the post-baptismal rites, and conse-quently a practical understanding of the rite, and finally a theology of confirmation: differing from the theology of baptism and subsequently justifying that development.

(b) A decisive factor for the development of a special rite was (of course against the background of the Augustinian theology of original sin and the necessity of baptism and the by now general practice of infant baptism) the western practice of according the bishops the privi-lege of administering the post-baptismal rites (increasinlgy delayed). There was a requirement of baptism of children at the earliest possible stage, usually by the presbyter, and as soon as possible the administra-tion of post-baptismal rites by the bishop: on the same day, or at least in the same week, or when the bishop could be reached, which could be a long drawn-out process. Now the bishop came to the confirmand (the starting point for the later 'confirmation visitation').

(c) The imparting to the bishops of the privilege of administering the post-baptismal rites did not presuppose two independent sacraments. On the contrary, the splitting up of the baptismal rite was at first considered abnormal. For a long time there were attempts to ensure that infant 'confirmation' followed infant baptism as soon as possible, as in the East. Only in the thirteenth century did resistance begin to cease, and was official notice taken of the actual position. A provincial council in Cologne in 1280 delayed 'confirmation' until at least the seventh year of age. Instead of a maximum a minimum limit was set. But, in accordance with ancient tradition, adults had to receive the post-baptismal rites immediately after baptism.

(d) Originally the post-baptismal rites were extremely simple, rather like the present-day baptismal anointing. Only from the ninth century was the extraordinary second baptismal anointing (signing with chrism), at first known only in Rome, developed into a closed 'rite of confirmation'. In the process, opening and closing prayers (all nevertheless determined by the baptismal liturgy) supply the theological motives for a now independent rite, which is nevertheless still conceived of in connection with baptism.

(e) What liturgy had long since practised was finally ratified by theology: first of all the theology of the high Middle Ages evolved a special theology — the 'theology of confirmation' — for subsequent justification of the now autonomous rite, which was to be administered by a bishop alone. The new theology sought to decide something very difficult to determine: the difference between 'confirmation' and baptism, the specific function, the salvific necessity, and the sign of this special rite.

(f) A homily stands at the beginning of this theology of confirmation: in the homily 'Advertamus' (thought to be the work of Faustus von Riez, for the first time in the history of theology a difference was asserted between baptism and confirmation. Without any connection with patristic tradition, it was claimed that in confirmation the Christian was strengthened for battle (confirmation as an arming of the Christian soldier), which meant an increase of grace in this life. That was extended by Aralar of Metz to an increase of glory in the next life.

(g) This still embryonic theology of confirmation produced by historical development was included in the *Decretum Gratiani*, which was basic to all medieval canon law. It entered it in the form of a series of confirmation canons which were falsely ascribed to various popes in such a way that confirmation was even treated — because it was reserved to the bishop — as a higher sacrament than baptism. Peter Lombard, the most annotated medieval theologian, accordingly characterized confirmation as a 'strengthening' gift of the Spirit ('ad robur' — in contradistinction to the gift of the Spirit in baptism 'ad remissionem'): a traditional formula right up to present-day scholastic text-books, but not grounded in the liturgy and theology of the first

century. Aquinas gave this theology of confirmation its ultimate traditional form by speculatively justifying, explaining and underwriting the circumstantially produced special rite. He did this mainly by means of the hitherto unknown analogy with physical life: the birth and growth of man until adulthood necessarily correspond in spiritual life to two sacraments: on the basis of two different ineradicable characteristics (baptismal and confirmation characters) we have two autonomous sacraments with two different effects of grace (the grace of baptism and the grace of confirmation). The medieval distinction between the two sacraments was then definitively confirmed by the Council of Florence in the Decree for the Armenians (1439), and confirmed by the Council of Trent against Luther (1547), without any further theological reflection, although the distinction of the two ritual ministers of the sacrament (a presbyter for baptism, and a bishop for confirmation) was in to the fore.

4. Indeterminate Nature of the Western Rite of Confirmation

(a) The 'matter' of the sacrament of confirmation is indefinite. It changes according to time and place. There is no continuity between the rite of the laying on of hands in Acts and the first witnesses of the episcopal laying on of hands in connection with baptism. The modern rite of confirmation originally descended not from Acts but the baptismal rites described by Tertullian and Hippolytus (laying on of hands, anointing, and signing with the cross), so that the result thereafter was an as yet clearly undecided competition between the laying on of hands and anointing (with signing).

(b) The post-baptismal laying on of hands to confer the Spirit was quite unknown in the Eastern Churches during the first centuries. The 'laying on of hands' which first appeared in connection with baptism in the West in the third century would seem to have been a stretching out of the right hand above those baptized (and therefore a prayer over the newly baptized), as found later, and right into the present century. Bishop Durandus's pontifical (+ 1296 and important for the subsequent period) requires the extension of both hands. Of course in Rome, since the twelfth century, a hand has been laid on each baptismal candidate separately. Precisely in the period in which the post-baptismal initiation rites were understood theologically as confirmation, the sealing with chrism moved into the foreground as the confirmation gesture proper. When in the fifteenth century Pope Innocent VIII generally prescribed the pontifical of Durandus, the laying on of hands gave way to anointing. As for Aquinas, so for the Council of Florence, 1439 (cf. Denz., 697), which was the authoritative norm against Luther as far as Trent was concerned, the anointing was the 'matter' of confirmation. Commenting on the texts in Acts, Thomas affirmed that the apostles had already anointed when laying on hands. Only in the eighteenth century did Benedict XIV try to resolve the difficulty by a compromise which still has legal validity in the Catholic Church. The individual laying on of hands was restored, but in such a way that during the signing with chrism the right hand is laid on the head of the confirmation candidate. This kind of cumulative rite admittedly contradicts the rite in Acts (the laying on of both hands) – formally as well. The main attempts to derive a post-baptismal laying-on of hands from the apostles are shown to be untenable. There is no question of a persistent tradition on this point.

(c) Post-baptismal anointing could be older in liturgico-historical terms than the post-baptismal laying on of hands. It occurs in the East as an alternative to the laying on of hands. In the West the development is dually conditioned: on the one hand by the specifically Roman practice of double anointing and its continuation in the non-Roman liturgy; on the other hand by the episcopal privilege of giving that second anointing, which becomes the core of the independent rite. In the high Middle Ages, anointing appears as the sole essential matter. The above-mentioned reintroduction of the individual laying on of hands in the eighteenth century does not bring with it a suppression of anointing. In fact it enjoys more continuity than the laying on of hands. But in this case there is absolutely no foundation in the New Testament. The spiritual anointing mentioned in the New Testament refers to baptism and not to any separate endowment with the Spirit. Hence the 'matter' of confirmation cannot be unequivocally determined (and certainly cannot be derived from Jesus Christ) as required by traditional sacramental theory.

(d) The 'form' of the sacrament of confirmation is not definite. The formula which was already known to Aquinas but which prevailed universally only at papal behest in the sixteenth century says nothing about the laying on of hands: 'Signo te signo crucis, et confirmo te chrismate salutis, in nomine Patris et Filii et Spiritus Sancti.' In the Middle Ages people believed in an apostolic origin of this formula. But the important term 'confirmo' entered the formula only at a relatively late date and, as a *terminus technicus* of Roman provenance, describes the post-baptismal rites as a whole. The formula in fact derives from early patristic times. But then it included no special endowment with the Spirit (nothing about strength, maturity or growth), but indirectly confirmed that the Spirit was received in baptism. It is justifiable to ask whether this formula was not originally merely a formula for baptismal anointing. The consistent and yet astonishingly indefinite formula easily hides the fact that the present-day rite of confirmation is an agglomeration of different, competing motifs and gestures: arising, by release from the baptismal context, as a result of

85

that episcopal privilege of the second post-baptismal anointing, which becomes increasingly emphasized in the formula in the course of time ('*Ego* signo . . .').

(e) With this kind of indefiniteness of sacramental matter and form, there is of course a similar lack of definition affecting the specific effect of confirmation: in spite of intensive efforts, theologians have not yet succeeded in identifying a specific sacramental 'grace' of confirmation differing in the bestowal of confirmation from that of baptism. Of course there are many descriptions and definitions of confirmation, but when they are not quite arbitrary they all apply equally to baptism: 'Completion', 'seal', 'putting on the armour of faith', 'the fulness of the Spirit' were not used in the ancient Church for a separate rite, but for baptism of water as the initiation rite pure and simple. A specific name came to be used for the additional rites, differing according to time and place) which were used together with baptism. The abovementioned development gave rise to a reservation of these terms (usual only from the Middle Ages onwards and even then not practised consistently) for a 'confirmation' separate from baptism, which marks those who are 'only' baptized as 'immature' in faith, would have seemed quite senseless to the centuries in which adult baptism was practised. The medieval theory of an autonomous 'character' of confirmation therefore cannot be derived from the patristic understanding of 'sphragis' ('signaculum'), since that refers the 'seal' to the Spirit, who is communicated in baptism. Not only the understanding of confirmation as the sacrament of maturity, of ripeness, of initiation into adulthood, manhood, or knighthood contradicts the early church understanding of baptism, but the similarly medieval definition of an autonomous sacrament in addition to baptism 'as *robur*': for strength in the struggle against inward and outward enemies, for courageous acknowledgment of faith in public, for martyrdom. All that was connected with baptism itself by the earlier Church — which in times of persecution certainly would not have kept quiet about a special sacrament for such purposes in addition to baptism. It would have found quite incomprehensible a special 'sacrament of the laity', of 'the universal priesthood', 'of lay ordination', 'of the lay apostolate', 'of Catholic action', which the theology of confirmation has discussed so energetically in the last few decades. That it is possible to subscribe to such an omnium-gatherum of diverse interpretations and effects which, apart from the very latest, can already be derived from baptism, and to do so without any clear criterion for one and the same confirmation, strengthens the impression that confirmation is not a sacrament in its own right alongside baptism.

(f) The *age* of the confirmand is indefinite. In the East the post-baptismal rites are still celebrated with baptism itself, and therefore usually over infants. In the West until some time in the thirteenth century at least officially the 'confirmation' of immature children was the predominant practice. But after the Fourth Lateran Council in 1215 had implicitly sanctioned a growing custom of putting off first Communion 'ad annos discretionis' (7-12, possibly 14-15 years of age), (cf. Denzinger 437), a parallel trend prevailed officially for confirmation (cf. the Cologne Provincial Council of 1218 with the requirement of a minimum age of 7, as stated later in the influential Catechism of the Council of Trent).

In the nineteenth century, however, the custom arose in various countries of confirming children not only at twelve and after but only *after* first Communion. The decree of Pius X on early Communion (1910) – even though it defines the 'aetas discretionis' as approximately seven years of age – strengthened the separation of baptism and confirmation (cf. Denzinger 2137-2144). Yet in this century there has been a determined emphasis on the tendency to confirm before first Communion, and thus to return to the ancient sequence of initiation. The situation was further complicated by a decree regarding confirmation issued under Pius XII in 1946, which reinstated infant confirmation in cases of need, so that children who died unconfirmed should not go without the 'augentum gloriae'. Because of this extremely contradictory development, it seems impossible to give any 'normal age' for confirmation.

(g) There is a similar lack of definition regarding the *minister* of confirmation. The reservation of the second post-baptismal anointing to the bishop was the original reason for the separation and then the chronological and spatial division of 'confirmation' from baptism. That is the impression gained from the particular emphasis with which the Councils of Florence and Trent define the bishop, and the bishop alone, as the ordinary minister (*minister ordinarius*) of confirmation. But the decree of 1946 on confirmation, which gave all priests and due representatives the power of confirming in cases of necessity, re-emphasized the question (which had always been a matter for discussion anyway), whether the episcopal privilege of confirmation concerned only a ruling of church law (and not therefore a *ius divinum*), and whether consequently every priest possessed a basic power of confirmation (even if a *potestas ligata*). Consideration of the practice of the Eastern Churches (and also of some instances in the earlier Latin Church) enabled Vatican II to correct the pronouncement which Trent declared anathema (Denzinger 967): The bishop is not the *minister ordinarius*, but only the *minister originarius* (the 'original' minister) of confirmation, so that the priest too can be a proper minister of confirmation (*Constitution on the Church*, art. 26). In addition, Vatican II corrected the apodictic Tridentine definition of the triad of bishops, priests and deacons

(traced back to 'divine design') (Denzinger 966: cf. 960), in the sense of the historically conditioned nature of that which has existed (art. 28). On the basis of the exegetico-historical findings indirectly referred to here, one can no longer escape admitting that in the New Testament *episcopes* or *presbyters* are either something different, or else no distinction is made between them. The division into three offices is not to be found in the New Testament, but for the first time in Ignatius of Antioch, when it is based on an historical development occurring initially in a Syriac setting. There appears to be no fundamental distinction between the ordination of a bishop and that of a priest. The present-day bishop is distinguished from the priest by his jurisdiction over a larger ecclesiastical area. A distinction in ecclesiastical law and discipline is possible and reasonable, but a theologico-dogmatic distinction on the other hand is unjustified and impossible. The episcopal privilege of confirmation is therefore – as was wholly appreciated in the earlier Church – purely a church law ruling.

Hence today we have seen a return to the origins. Progress in theology and the Church has ultimately and finally revealed as questionable that process which led to a separation of 'confirmation' from baptism – with all the consequences regarding 'matter', 'form', 'effect', 'minister' and 'recipient'. Hence the way has finally been opened up for a new consideration of the matter, and possibly a new arrangement.

II. CONFIRMATION AS UNFOLDING, ASSURANCE AND COMPLETION OF BAPTISM

If we are at long last to arrive at a theologically exact, conclusive and convincing solution of the difficulties which have burdened discussion of the subject for so long, then the exegetical and historical findings, instead of being constantly patched up with apologetics, must be taken seriously in theory and practice, and turned to good ends. Various viewpoints occur in this regard which can only be summarized. For a positive solution, I would refer the reader to the book by J. Amougou-Atangana, which deals more exhaustively with problems which can only be touched on in this paper.

1. The Reference of Confirmation to Baptism

(a) Exegetical and historical data support the basic fact that *the present-day rite of confirmation developed from the baptismal rite*. The confirmation rite is historically and concretely a part, an aspect, a phase of the one initiation which was completed with baptism in the Church from the start. Without baptism there is no confirmation. But on the other hand baptism was and is possible – according to quite traditional teaching – without confirmation. Confirmation is not necessary – and this too is part of traditional doctrine – for the salvation of the individual Christian.

(b) If confirmation is still to have any meaning today – which is yet to be discussed – then it is only *in strict connection with baptism*: in connection with baptism, ·and in development, confirmation and completion of baptism. If there is no connection with baptism, then the significance and practical framework of confirmation are delivered up to wholly arbitrary ends, as is richly evidenced in the various medieval and contemporary interpretations and attempts at reform. But theological theory and pastoral practice have to fit together.

(c) Therefore confirmation cannot be understood as a quite separate sacrament. It is no autarchic and autonomous sacrament independent of baptism. Confirmation cannot be placed on the same footing as baptism: neither by argument from New Testament evidence, nor from its relationship with the preaching and activity of Jesus, nor from the clarity and precision of the outward sign, nor from the clarity and precision of content and meaning. At Trent, in spite of Luther's questioning, there was no awareness of the complex exegetical and historical data in this·regard. But when confirmation is seen in its original connection with baptism, then the question of an institution of confirmation by Christ is automatically solved, whereby the analogicity (if not equivocity) of the concept of a sacrament used at Trent is once more apparent. Then it is possible to characterize confirmation as a subsidiary sacrament sharing in baptism (which, together with the Eucharist, is a main sacrament).

(d) In contradistinction therefore to the distinction sometimes adduced as a way out – 'baptism in Christ, confirmation in the Spirit', and to similar artificial distinctions, we have to stress the point: baptism like confirmation is concerned with one and the same Christ, one and the same Spirit, one and the same grace, and one and the same faith.

(e) If confirmation has a meaning it is as the ultimate phase of the one rite of initiation. That means: in as clear as possible and chronological connection with baptism, but in any case before admission to the Eucharist. Admission to the eucharistic celebration and community presupposes initiation – whether in one or two phases. Historically, concretely and pastorally the sequence is only as it was until the nineteenth century: baptism – confirmation – Eucharist. Whoever represents a logical relationship between theory and practice cannot first accept the connection between baptism and confirmation (confirmation as the closing phase and completion of initiation) in theory, then arbitrarily decide the right sequence of the sacrament, and deny that relationship in practice. If the Eucharist is a sacrament of the initiated, which no one contests, and on the other hand confirmation has to do with initiation, which would seem to be incontestable, then it is quite illogical to carry out confirmation only after the reception of the Eucharist.

(f) The meaningfulness of confirmation cannot be presupposed as obvious but has to be reconsidered under present-day conditions. If, as in the past, adult baptism were a control instance, the problem would appear differently: then there would hardly be any more reason to separate baptism and certain post-baptismal rites. Initiation could occur in a single action as in the ancient Church and today in the Eastern Churches. The same would be true if the Churches all rejected infant baptism and took up the baptism of children in the broader sense (in the early school years) or decided on adult baptism proper. But for the moment that appears improbable. It is not a good idea to try to solve tomorrow's problems too far in advance, when we can't see beyond today's difficulties. It is appropriate to consider confirmation today on the presupposition of the infant baptism current in all the major Churches (despite all criticisms of it). Historically, we can see that the post-baptismal rites are not an obvious consequence of infant baptism, as the development in the Eastern Churches shows clearly. But they *could* develop from infant baptism — if the bishops reserved certain rites for themselves. The reason for the autonomy of confirmation was the reservation of privilege by the bishops. But the factual requirement for that reservation was infant baptism.

2. Infant Baptism as Incomplete Baptism

(a) Just as the Baptists at the time of the Reformation, so today critics (especially since Karl Barth's adverse remarks) find infant baptism justifiably questionable, because immature infants seem to lack what is a *conditio sine qua non* of baptism: the act of faith. Whoever cannot hear the word cannot answer it in faith. The requirement of concrete belief carries with it the requirement of a voluntary Church (in contradistinction to a national Church).

(b) Opposed to the requirement of concrete faith are the scholastic conception of the inpouring of an unconscious *habitus* of faith and Luther's idea of an infant faith, yet they are in no way convincing, but rather ungrounded hypotheses.

(c) The dispute cannot be decided from a New Testament basis. To be sure, baptism as evidenced might well have included entire 'houses' (families — analogously to the Jewish baptism and circumcision of proselytes). But on the other hand nowhere in the New Testament is there any mention of infant baptism. In 1 Cor. 7.14, where the children of Christian parents are called 'holy' only by reason of their parentage without any mention of a baptism, infant baptism would appear to be a possibility at best for the children of converts. Only with the emphasis on infant baptism at the beginning of the second century, so the argument runs, was a baptism of all children imposed. From the basis of the New Testament, the decisive question is not whether there were *de facto* infant baptisms in the New Testament period, but whether infant baptism is in any way demonstrable from the New Testament.

(d) A false argument for infant baptism (though one current for a long time past) is this: without infant baptism there is no salvation. Church tradition is not univocal on this point. The Greek Fathers like the older Latin Fathers recognize no *limbo puerorum*, but incline more to the salvation of the unbaptized. Only the late Augustine, on the basis of his dispute with Pelagius and his novel doctrine of original sin, condemned unbaptized children to hell. This rigorous idea was continually toned down from the early Middle Ages: from Anselm to Thomas — so that hell became a pre-hell and the pre-hell eventually turned into a pre-heaven (natural happiness without the divine vision). Today that kind of *limbus puerorum* is largely rejected as in no way demonstrable from the New Testament and as contradictory to the general divine will of redemption; and (also in the course of a revision of Augustine's original sin theory) the possibility of salvation for unbaptized children is also accepted.

(e) Of course the rejection of infant baptism brings big difficulties with it which cannot be taken lightly in view of the centuries-old and weighty tradition of the Eastern and Western Churches.

i. A shifting of baptism to adulthood would leave the fundamental significance of baptism for the Christian life and community in the background, and accordingly emphasize personal fidelity and reflection on it.

ii. The point in time at which the young person is enough of a believer to be baptized, would be difficult to decide in practice and in its turn would require some kind of general rule. Probably it would have to be left to psychologists to determine whether faith is adequate in the seventh or only in the thirtieth year of life.

iii. A decision of faith for baptism taken once and for all in the ancient Christian sense presupposes a particular situation of conversion which could be introduced only artificially in a still externally Christian society. In families (more or less) permeated by Christianity, becoming a Christian doesn't take place as a unique, conscious, decisive moment, but as a gradual transition from a dependent and non-reflective to a personal and autonomous belief.

iv. In the case of adult baptism, a large number of churchgoers, namely young people, would be unbaptized persons (heathen), who as such would perhaps have to be excluded for more than ten years, if not

91

from divine service itself, then from the core of the Christian divine service: that is, participation in the eucharistic meal. They would be second-class churchgoers in a Church which from the beginning was intended to be a eucharistic community. This unfortunate situation has led some Baptist parishes to create a substitute rite for infant baptism, which in its turn is performed at the expense of baptism as the Christian sacrament of initiation and as the fundamental Christian sacrament.

v. Therefore it is not only a product of the conception of the national Church that up to now the requirement of adult baptism has been unable to make headway as the only legitimate form of baptism in the Christian Churches.

(f) A properly grounded infant baptism cannot be ruled out from the start as unjustifiable by New Testament evidence. Three points are usually cited; they may also be seen as three aspects of a single answer:

i. God's gracious call precedes human faith. Infant baptism bears witness to the fact that God already blesses this little being, that God has called him to salvation, and that the decision of faith is to be understood only as an answer to God's action.

ii. The child does not stand alone but in the living family context. Infant baptism expresses the fact that children belong to their parents spiritually as well, and that therefore they are called with them to the same end and are already 'hallowed'. The Church does not baptize children abstractly and individualistically, but as sons and daughters of these Christian parents (from which of course practical conclusions have to be drawn in regard to the desire, preparation and readiness of parents for Christian education).

iii. Infant baptism intends one to believe and confess one's belief. In infant baptism the necessary relation between faith and baptism, which does not have to be a chronological coincidence, is expressed in that baptism destines one to believe, aims at belief, and awaits belief. God's Yes to man requires man's Yes to God. If belief is not the significant core of baptism, the infant baptism is pointless. Only when the believer grasps the meaning of baptism does infant baptism reach its goal. Until that point the parents (and the godparents only in second place) who want the child to be baptized, who make the confession of faith, and who promise that it will receive a Christian education, are the representatives of the child, so that in this respect at least there is a certain conjunction of (representative) faith and baptism. But only when the baptized individual himself acknowledges the baptism which his parents wished him to receive, does baptism find the wholeness and completion of adult baptism.

(g) Consequently, if infant baptism can be fundamentally demonstrated from a New Testament basis and is in practical terms the

preferred solution, nevertheless that does not mean that it is in any way the ideal case of baptism as intended by the New Testament. Theologically speaking, even though it is the normal instance, it is a borderline case. Without the fulfilment of faith in practice, infant baptism remains a torso: civil rights in the church community as it were by proxy, and real proxy, but not fully acknowledged. Hence infant baptism is a defective form of baptism. It is a non-concluded, incomplete baptism which itself requires completion, fulfilment in the real belief and confession of faith of the baptized person. It is in this respect that confirmation finds its location and meaning both traditionally and in terms of the present situation.

III. THE MEANING OF CONFIRMATION

1) Historically and factually, the meaning of confirmation is un-equivocally to be found in the development, assurance, confirmation and completion of baptism. Phenomenologically, confirmation marks the point — naturally in a long, complex process of development — at which the child, baptized at the wish of believing parents, now, after a fundamental catechesis appropriate to its age, publicly acknowledges its baptism and confesses its faith before the community, in order to be recognized in a special rite as a full member of the church community by a representative of that community, and to be accepted and allowed entrance to the community's eucharistic meal. Hence confirmation and first communion would take place in the same process of celebration.

2) Confirmation understood in this way guarantees the funda-mental connection with baptism and yet, in contradistinction to baptism, has its own significance and function. The basic inadequacies of infant baptism are thereby repaired and confirmation is made more obviously meaningful.

The call of God, which was proclaimed on behalf of the child in baptism, is now consciously acknowledged by the young person and public responsibility is taken for it.

The faith which the parents confessed as representatives of the child and which was only cited in expectancy in the child's baptism, is now actually present as a freely acknowledged, self-responsible, publicly confessed decision of the young person to direct his life according to the standard of the gospel of Jesus Christ.

The baptism which initially was received only passively by the child, is now effective in active acceptance of the offer of grace in the open belief, confession and action of the young person. The Spirit appealed to as taking effect in baptism now becomes an existentially decisive reality for the faith and life of the young person.

The reception into the Church which was then given basically to the immature infant in baptism and formally acknowledged is now ratified solemnly in accordance with the public declaration of agreement on the part of the young person, and realized in practice by admission to the eucharistic meal (the consequences in canon law for membership of the Church, its rights and duties, would have to be reconsidered on this bases).

3) This view of confirmation avoids both a medieval and objectivistic sacramentalism which expects confirmation to impart a special grace, and thereby miraculous results for this or for the 'other' world, and for that reason even recommends a special infant confirmation. At the same time, however, it avoids that kind of enlightened but subjectivistic intellectualism which takes an ethical view of confirmation, and sees it mainly as the conclusion of a process of instruction (Sunday school, moral education), and as something like a rite of civic maturity or a Christian initiation into communal virtues. In confirmation as in baptism itself, there must always be an 'objective' aspect (the actual granting of salvation as an action of the Spirit) alongside the 'subjective' aspect (its human correspondence). Confirmation will only be understood as an adjunct to baptism if it is seen as the personal appropriation of spiritual action.

4) In this synthetic (objective-subjective) perspective, the word 'confirmation', 'con-firmatio' can be understood more appropriately, while taking into account a number of traditional emphases:

(a) as the ('subjective') confirmation of the faith to which baptism commits, and which is now accepted by the baptized person in his own responsibility and free commitment, and publicly acknowledged before the community;

(b) as an ('objective') strengthening of the baptized person, who at this moment believes and publicly confesses his faith, through the Holy Spirit received in baptism and newly effective in actual faith.

5) It should then be more clearly apparent what is intended in the definition of confirmation as development, affirmation and completion of the spiritual action of baptism.

(a) Development: Confirmation is not an independent sacrament alongside baptism. It is rather — historically and factually — a continuation and development of baptism: the concluding phase of the baptismal initiation. Therefore it is — like baptism — unrepeatable. Not because of some sacramental 'character of confirmation', but because of participation in baptism and its unrepeatability.

(b) Affirmation: As a development of baptism, however, confirmation is not an extension, repetition or surpassing of a baptism which is complete in itself.

It is instead a recognition and ratification of the baptism that has already taken place. God's call has been made. The Spirit has been imparted, the baptism is valid, reception by the church community is irrevocable, and to that the person receiving baptism makes his free and public act of assent.

(c) Completion: As development and affirmation of baptism, therefore, confirmation is not only a formal ceremony of acknowledgment or a bureaucratic rite of reception. It is rather a conscious acceptance in present belief, in public confession, of an effective renewal of the spiritual event of baptism, and as such the last stage of the grounding of the Christian life which is to be played out and proven thereafter. It is a completion therefore both in regard to the event of baptism itself and in regard to the faith which definitively and publicly accepts that baptismal event. It is a completion therefore which can be only the beginning and not the end of that Christian life which after confirmation as well is endangered by weakness, doubt, temptation and disbelief, but which in spite of all dangers can be lived in the power of the Spirit of Jesus Christ.

IV. THE PRACTICE OF CONFIRMATION

1. Express Reference to Baptism

The historically and theologically established reference of confirmation to baptism must also be expressed in the practical shape of the rite. The following are worth consideration:

(a) The repetition of specific formulas from infant baptism comprehensible for adults and children: especially the repetition of the baptismal questions and answers and a simple confession of faith which emphasizes the following of Christ.

(b) During confirmation the parents should stand at the children's side. The baptismal godparents should also be the confirmation sponsors.

(c) The reference to the practice of the Christian life required in baptism (indicative – imperative, gift – task, reception of the Spirit – living spiritually) should permeate the whole confirmation rite. There must be a real introduction to the lived following of Christ.

2. Age

Suggestions are made for varying ages between one and thirty years. The question of the right age for confirmation is however only debated to such an extent because the theological premises are not precisely stated first of all, and an attempt is made to replace theological reasoning with dogmatic (medieval or modern) prejudices, psychological and educational arguments, personal feelings and subjective opinions.

Of course in regard to confirmation there is a certain area of free movement for pastoral judgment. But if theory and practice are not to conflict, the following must be taken into consideration:

(a) No infant confirmation. The same objections can be raised against infant confirmation as against infant baptism, and to a greater degree, since the deficiency of infant confirmation increases the deficiency of infant baptism. At the same time, in a theologically indefensible way, infant confirmation would insinuate that confirmation was necessary for salvation, or that it was an 'increase' of 'grace' or of heavenly bliss. That does not imply a condemnation of eastern practice, since in that case the post-baptismal anointing administered with baptism from the beginning never had the significance of a separate, independent sacrament (with a specifically distinct 'grace' in the Latin sense).

(b) Confirmation before admission to the Eucharist. This is the obvious result of everything that has been said on the cohesion of theory and practice and on confirmation as the last phase of baptismal initiation, which for its part is orientated to the goal of admission to the Eucharist. Connection with baptism implies confirmation as soon as possible after baptism, and in any case confirmation before admission to the Eucharist. If confirmation is freed from reference to baptism and orientation to the Eucharist, it is possible arbitrarily to decide on almost any age as proper for confirmation, and then of course to underpin it ideologically: not only the age of maturity ('sacrament of maturity'), but civic maturity, middle age ('sacrament of responsibility'), the climacteric ('sacrament of complete maturity') or pensionable age ('sacrament of retirement'), or even death ('sacrament of perseverance'). In a theological perspective, all these attempts are improper solutions. Psychologically and educationally too, no one is hardly more justifiable than any other. Here we need not subjective reasoning but arguments.

(c) Puberty and adolescence are hardly suitable for confirmation for psychological, educational and pastoral reasons. To summarize the very real difficulties a few heads are appended: the onset of conscious sexuality, turning inwards (experience of ego-consciousness) and contradictory behaviour (conflict) to external authorities (parents, home, school, church), internalization of religiousness, and rejection of religious professions and formal rites; stress because of major life decisions in vocation and training, marriage and family (often connected with change of locality); pastoral difficulties with personal judgment under heavy fluctuation; actual exclusion of a large number of young people from confirmation, the consequent danger of a two-class Christianity, and so on. In this connection serious consideration has to be given not only to the worries and negative experiences of priests in regard to earlier 'religious education' (something similar would be

necessary for preparation for confirmation), but particularly the syndrome that accompanies the Protestant confirmation at the age of maturity: admission to Communion comes too late, the baptized aren't incorporated into the parish, the result is to a large extent non-parish Christianity (confirmation is virtually confirmation 'out of' the Church).

(d) Not only the theologically grounded connection and chronological relation between confirmation and baptism, but suasions of developmental psychology recommend confirmation in the early years of school (before admission to the Eucharist): at this time the child is already capable of learning in a way appropriate to him what Christ means for him. At the same time he is at a stage of uncomplicated openness, which makes him accessible to a large extent to religious education and an extension of knowledge, and especially ready for witness, example and action. In the New Testament the child (in his way a complete man, as modern developmental psychology emphasizes) is offered as an exemplar of the attitude of faith.

3. The Need for a Basic Catechesis which is Appropriate to the Age of the Individual

A child is only able to accustom himself to faith if the Christian message is given to him in the correct way, appropriate to his age. Here the parents, their attitude and behaviour as a whole, have a strong mediating function from earliest childhood, as psychoanalysis has shown. Child religious education on the other hand has the task of offering a didactic and reflective introduction to Christianity. This should not take the form of an isolated instruction about confession and Communion in the old way, nor that of a theoretical rehearsal in memorizable 'propositions' but should be a fundamental catechesis grounded in the New Testament and according with the particular context and practice. It should, by using the various methods and media of modern instructional techniques, show the child what man's destiny is, what God and Jesus mean for him in his life, and how a man can live and act meaningfully, but also suffer and die, in accordance with Jesus's example, always supported by God and serving his fellow men. Then, after one or two years of fundamental catechesis, the child would be prepared to say Yes definitively and publicly to Jesus, in order to be received as a full member of the church community and admitted to its eucharistic meal. Then confirmation would follow directly on 'first Communion'.

4. New Form of the Rite

(a) In view of the historically demonstrated concurrence of the laying on of hands and anointing, in the rite preference should

97

certainly be given to the laying on of hands, even when anointing is not definietly excluded. The laying on of hands is taken from the Old Testament (cf. Moses in Num. 27.18-23). For the New Testament it appears in the rite of ordination as — together with prayer — the visible sign of the Holy Spirit called down on man. That corresponds to our idea of confirmation as a development, affirmation and completion of the spiritual process of baptism, and even today is quite understandable. At the same time (and here the well-known passages in Acts are relevant) it expresses the ecclesial dimension: a definitively recognized reception into the Christian community. Anointing could be reserved for baptism alone.

(b) The formula accompanying the laying on of hands should clearly express the meaning of confirmation, and especially the reference to baptism (for example: 'Receive in the Holy Spirit the completion of baptism and be a true and faithful member of the community of Jesus Christ'). The previous confession of faith in the baptismal rite would be an integral part of the rite.

(c) In addition, the rite of confirmation (if it has not already taken place) should be cleansed of unbiblical, historically outdated and unreal elements: that applies on the one hand to certain theologically problematical prayer formulas, on the other to certain additional rites such as those adopted since the thirteenth century: for instance the slap on the cheek, only included since the thirteenth century and only now discarded, which was adopted from German symbolism and was intended to impress on the memory important events and facts — in this case the unrepeatability of confirmation. The laying on of one hand combined with anointing and a pronouncement should be replaced by the laying on of both hands. Finally, in connection with the newly prescribed rite, notions such as the spiritual relationship between godfather and godchild, traditionally connected with confirmation, should be discarded or revised.

5. The Minister

(a) The question of the minister of confirmation is, as we have seen, not essentially dogmatic but a question of pastoral expediency and the corresponding canon law.

(b) At present, however, it is unfortunately a fact that long 'confirmation trips' through a diocese often keep bishops from more important duties, from ministering to ministers, and pastoral visitation of parishes, and in certain circumstances give them an illusory impression of having achieved 'contact with the people'.

(c) On account of the significance of a correctly understood rite of confirmation, and for the sake of emphasizing the context of the Church as a whole (admission to membership not merely of the individual parish, but of the Church of a city, region and diocese), confirmation should not as a rule be administered by the local parish priest. It should meaningfully represent to candidates the Church as including but surpassing the individual parish.

(d) Normally, then, confirmation is best administered by someone holding ecclesial office: someone, that is, who combines liturgical and pastoral functions. If instead of ordinaries diocesan cities had local bishops (as in the ancient Church) in every regional centre, who, under the leadership of the diocesan bishop (= metropolitan), coordinated the pastoral work of the region, and undertook certain liturgical functions, then confirmation could be administered once a year by such local bishops. In the present set-up, in most dioceses (from the viewpoint of status), the deacon would be the most suitable minister of confirmation. Emphasis should always be laid on the celebratory aspects (confirmation and first Communion).

In this article I have tried to develop a consistent theological presentation of the functional aspect of confirmation. In certain details it is debatable, but as a whole it is, I trust, grounded on a firm exegetical and historical basis. I have written out of respect for the decisive features of mainline Catholic tradition, and in answer to the critical objections of the Reformers, while keeping in mind theologically responsible and practicable solutions in the contemporary Church.

Translated by John Maxwell

Notes

1   Cf. E. Schillebeeckx, *De sacramentele Heilseconomie. Theologische bezinning op S. Thomas' sacramentenleer in het licht van de traditie en van de hedendaags sacramentenproblematiek* (Antwerp, 1952); *id.*, Art. 'Virnsel', in *Theologisch Woodenbork*, ed., H. Brink III (Roermond, 1958), col. 4840-69; *id.*, *Christ the Sacrament* (London, 1963).
2   This article is based on my lectures on the sacraments given at Tübingen in 1964/5, 1967, and 1969, at Basle in 1969, and at Princeton Theological Seminary, 1970. I also gave a summary lecture on confirmation to the Basle diocesan council in Olten in 1969, which was circulated in duplicated form.
3   The complex of problems in this regard has been exegetically, historically and systematically examined in detail by a student of mine, J. Amougou-Atangana, in *Ein Sakrament des Geistempfangs? Zum Verhältnis von Taufe und Firmung. Ökumenische Forschungen*, third sacramentological section, vol. 1 (Freiburg, 1974), to which reference should be made for citations, bibliography, and so on. It has been of great value to me in the historical establishment of these theses.
4   The continuing debate on infallibility has as yet prevented me from completing my work on the sacraments undertaken as a sequel to *The Church.*

HEALING AND THE SPIRIT

Editorial

Gasiano Floristan

Christian Experience and Therapy

A series of 'disruptive revisions', nearly always stemming from attacks by the great atheists of contemporary culture, has been a continuing feature of Christianity from the last century onwards. The 'masters of suspicion' — Feuerbach, Marx, Nietzsche and Freud — have placed religion on trial in their radical critique of the culture of their time. Their different approaches have the common aim of 'throwing light on the power of man, displaced and lost in an alien transcendence'.[1] Nevertheless, the judgment that Marx and Frued, in particular, are 'materialistic atheists and enemies of all religion' today needs modifying 'from many points of view'.[2]

This issue does not set out to undertake this sort of modification directly, but indirectly this is at least part of its import. The authors are tackling directly the issue of Christian experience and therapy, set in the context of the wider dialogue between psychoanalysis and faith.

To put it mildly, the history of the relationship between psycho-analysis and religion, from the early development of the sciences of psychology, and even more since Freud, has been one of mutual distrust. Nevertheless, the similarities between the two have become far more apparent in recent years, and there has been a mutual drawing together, as the articles in this issue indicate.[3]

So as not to lose ourselves in the complexities of the relationships between faith and psychoanlysis, and in view of the fact that our basic concern is with the equally extensive and complex field of spirituality, we begin by concentrating on a concern that is both human and religious: healing. This is studied from the theological aspect by Mongillo, and from the therapeutic aspect by Rossi. Even if an inter-disciplinary expertise is not always absolute in these articles, at least the authors who write from the background of theological discipline

103

show an extensive knowledge of and a fine sensitivity to psychology, and the same is equally true vice-versa.

The juxtaposition of Christian experience and therapy does not imply either an ingenuous concordism or that there is an abyss separating the two, which are both experiences affecting believers as well as those who accept modern rationalism. This issue tackles the question of whether therapy in general or particular present-day forms of it affect Christian experience either favourably or unfavourably, and the opposite question: whether Christian experience in general or particular forms of it involve therapeutic or neurotic processes. In view of existing rivalries, we are obviously not taking the part of any particular school of psychoanlysis, nor do we assume that the term 'therapy' can be limited to any particular form of application. To limit the field a little, however, we are confining our examination to psychological or psychosomatic therapies, always considered in relation to Christian experience.

If scientific honesty, as well as a basic Christian approach, obliges us to leave many points unresolved, it seems clear that this particular question forces this situation, which is certainly preferable to defensive or offensive polemic, which here would be even more of an aberration than usual.[4]

There are of course certain starting points, based on both religious (in this case Christian), and therapeutic (here generally psychoanalytical, and mainly Freudian) experiences. Two theologians tackle the therapeutic aspect of Christianity (Fierro) and of spirituality (Castillo). In other words, both posit answers to the question of whether faith and Christian life produce therapeutic results.

The obverse of this question is whether psychotherapy can have religious or irreligious results. Christians approach psychoanalysis from a whole range of viewpoints, and their image of it is constantly changing. Once believers admit the experience of psychoanalysis, its effects are evident in their life of faith. This is also seen in a traditional practice at present undergoing a deep transformation, that of spiritual direction, and in another widespread modern practice: group therapy.

We also offer pieces on specific themes: Jesus as healer (Kahlefeld) and the phenomenon of healing in the pentecostal movement (Combet and Fabre).

There are many aspects of the relationship between therapy and Christian experience, with some constant features running through all. The reader will be able to discern these as he reads through this issue: his personal experience is his most valuable guide — in the best psychoanalytic theory and in the best Christian tradition.

Translated by Paul Burns

Notes

1   Cf. P. Ricoeur, 'The Atheism of Freudian Psychoanalysis', *Concilium* (1966).
2   Cf. E. Fromm, 'Reflections on Religion and Religiosity', *Concilium* (1972).
3   Cf. A. de Waelhens, 'Traces of the Image of Man in Psychoanalysis', *Concilium* (1973).
4   Cf. L. Beirnaert, 'Psychoanalytical Theory and Moral Evil', *Concilium* (1973).

Georges Combet   Laureat Fabre

The Pentecostal Movement and the Gift of Healing

THERE are long processes of maturation in spiritual life, the hard, patient road trod by the people of God in the desert; there are also sudden conversions, unexpected deliverances, the breakthrough into the promised land . . . There are long convalescences, lasting a whole life-time and a whole death; there are also blind men who one morning open their eyes to find they can see, paralytics who leap suddenly to their feet. Healings happen. A people can wait patiently for its saviour to appear, and then a virgin bears a child.

The gift of healing challenges us in the very core of our Christian existence, where the continuity of our hope and the breakthrough of our faith find their joint expression. Yet in the cultural and religious world we know, in which we live and by which we are impregnated, the gift of healing has acquired a bad name. Our rationalistic minds, our psychological reactions, certain interpretations of Scripture . . . all these teach us to stand back from and distrust all that the gift of heal-ing brings with it: fideism, fundamentalism, religious sentimentality, an often morbid attachment to the unusual. This reaction is also in a way a sensible one to the past of the Church, when the distinction between faith and the sort of naive credulity that can well produce spiritual and psychological disorders has not always been made.

And yet the facts are there . . .

Not only is healing a subject of discussion, which is a first fact that cannot be ignored, but healings indubitably occur, which is a second fact (not necessarily connected with the first). And, for a third fact, there is a close correlation between the evangelical texts that speak of healing and present-day accounts: the same spiritual approach centred on forgiveness of sins and faith, the importance of an actual physical gesture, the confession of Jesus as the saviour, and the fact that healing is a sign for those who believe, and a sign of contradiction for those who do not. This is not the place to set up a verbal office of proof, *a la* Lourdes, but one has to state the fact that all sorts of psychological and physical illnesses have been arrested in their course, either progressively or suddenly, through the exercise of charism. Psychological illnesses are the commonest, but there are many cases of physical illnesses that have been pronounced incurable and that have yet been cured for reasons that the present state of our medical knowledge is powerless to explain. The purpose of this article is not to document such cures (see the two books by Kathryn Kuhlman and the case-studies collected by Agnes Sandford for this), but rather to attempt an internal examination of the course indicated by the rediscovery of spiritual gifts in general and the gift of healing in particular by the Church. If we are to approach this gift without too much risk of false interpretation, we need to place it in the long and varied current of charismatic renewal.

For several years now most Christian confessions have been invaded by a spiritual current unprecedented in history. Christians of all Churches are coming together to pray, to re-discover the mainspring of all Christian life together. 'Charismatic renewal', 'neo-Pentecostalism', 'Renewal in the Spirit', 'Catholic Pentecostalism' . . . these are all facets of a renewal that shares a number of features with earlier periods of Church history, and some of their dangers: illuminism, sectarianism . . . But it also manifests some of the strong points of any genuine spiritual renewal: a rediscovery of the Word, of the life of faith, an openness to the poor, apostolic zeal, a sense of prayer. Other aspects are frankly new and lead one to believe that we are witnessing an important step forward – a definitive one, some would say – in the life of the Church. And yet what appears most new is in fact what is oldest: the re-discovery of charisms and spiritual gifts. One has to read the Epistles of Paul and the Acts of the Apostles to understand what is happening today: they speak of the gifts of the Spirit, and include the gift of healing among them.

I. RESISTANCE TO GIFTS

It is not easy for us to accept the existence of such a gift. Everything in us rebels against it. We are not really disposed to allow God to act like this in us or through us. The prestige we attach to human intelligence, the need we feel to explain the whole of reality rationally, the amazing progress made by medicine . . . everything predisposes us to reject what seems to short-circuit the logical processes of mediation we establish ourselves. Faced with the very real risks of acquiring an unhealthy taste for magic and the miraculous, we fall into the opposite trap, which is sometimes worse than the first: refusing to believe the evidence of every-day occurrences, forgetting that everything is a gift of God; it is not difficult to believe in miracles, what is difficult is to believe in the ordinary, daily fact of the love of God in our lives. Contrary to what many people believe, spiritual gifts have a distinct flavour of the ordinary about them: far from leading us away from the world and its natural laws, they invite us to contemplate and participate in the mystery of the incarnation, of the prodigiously ordinary alliance between God and man in the form of Jesus Christ.

The Wise Men did not know where to go to pay homage to the King of the Jews. A document provided by specialists set them on their way. But it was not a prince in a palace they found, it was a poor kid in a stable. Mary did not know where they had put him to whom she wanted to pay her last respects; her name whispered by a stranger she took for the gardener brought about recognition. She came to look for a dead man, but embraced a living one. The Samaritan woman did not know which mountain she should climb to worship God properly; a tired Jew who asked her for a little water showed her the right way: 'The hour is coming, and we are living in it, when true worshippers will worship the Father in the Spirit of truth.' She was expecting a prodigious Messiah, but it was an act of faith that showed her the Saviour.

The ways are different, but the discovery has a common feature everywhere: each one finds something quite other than what he imagined. The Wise Men expected to find a prince in a downy cradle and found an ordinary baby tucked into a manger. Mary expected to find a corpse and instead found the warmth of a loved one. The Samaritan woman dreamt of a super-star Messiah but it was only her faith that showed his saving power.

Prayer groups are now attracting more and more people; many are seeking without knowing what they will find. Some are drawn by a taste for the marvellous, others are seeking a God to hide in, and it is true that prayer is sometimes the way out of taking action that one fears. The rest, those on their way, simply accept that they will be disconcerted by the Spirit who leads both within and without. Little by little they discover the essential to lie elsewhere, at once much closer to them, since they have to love their brothers who are with them, and much farther from them, since the breath of the Spirit breathes to the rhythm of the Universe. There can be nothing more ordinary than learning to breathe; prayer is the breath of life. Dying on the Cross, Christ gave up his Spirit to us as well as to his Father, that Spirit which is the creative breath that can raise the dead. It is perhaps not surprising that in this time of crisis, when faith is ailing, the Holy Spirit brings about true cures while teaching us to pray, to breathe. Renewal groups also possess a certain prudence and wisdom with regard to cures: free from the rather unpleasant attitudes of certain sects who brandish cures as an apologetic weapon, they give thanks to the Lord for demonstrating his effective love in this way, and if necessary bear witness to the event as something that has changed a whole life. This is a normal part of Christian life.

But many of us have not reached this point, and our resistance to this life of the Spirit in us can show itself in various ways. The first is simply to deny his activity, or relativize it out of existence. Many biblical passages can be robbed of their meaning, carefully avoided, or dismissed as inconvenient in this way. The second, and more usual, way is to limit the sphere of the Spirit's activity — to censure him, in effect. We believe him to be at work in the Universe, we believe him to be capable of changing men's hearts, of opening them to God, but we do not really believe that man is a true whole so that God's action in him can not only free him from his sins, but also cure him of his illnesses.

Whatever the reasons for our resistance, the fact is that most of the time we not only do not aspire to the spiritual gifts (1 Cor. 12.31), but consciously or unconsciously reject them. And that is enough — God respects us to such an extent that he will not force his gifts on us. He who does not want or ask will not receive!

II. RE-LEARNING THE GESTURES OF FAITH

Many Christians feel ill-at-ease with any sort of prayer of petition. While there are many reasons for this unease, they nearly all stem from a lack of faith that makes prayer impossible. This is where the hearing of the impossible prayer takes on its full significance for the individual and for the Church. What matters is not a particular healing, nor that it should be an extraordinary one that amazes the doctors, nor even that it should be an apparently quite ordinary one; what matters is that the Holy Spirit, in the depressed and disorganized context of present-day loss of faith, is patiently teaching us the gestures of faith.

Those of us who are bound up in political, family, cultural and other activities can hardly conceive the extent to which prayer in itself demands the total commitment of the whole person. Most of those who move in the ambit of the charismatic renewal movements regard a request to the whole community to pray for their conversion as an important step. The words and gestures (laying on of hands) that accompany this very personal and at the same time very communitary

109

prayer are simple, but this simplicity clothes a very important require-ment: if we really commit ourselves to asking the Spirit of the Lord to come upon us, to purify us (Lk. 11.13), to send us to our brothers, we will not do so in vain. For many Christians this step is not under-taken without deep fear, and the expression 'baptism in the Spirit', even if it can be misunderstood, well expresses this experience of plunging in, drowning, death and resurrection. This is the situation whose logic provides the context for the renewal of charisms in the Church. They are effectively given, but at the same time they must be welcomed. Not only, as is very clear from the gospel accounts, must the conversion of those who are healed by a first-fruit of their cure, but also for those who exercise the gift of healing, there is a whole course in faith, a long apprenticeship required. Faith alone is not enough; dis-cernment is needed too. In this sphere, more than in any other, errors can have grave consequences.

With great wisdom, those who exercise this gift or ministry of heal-ing (such as Agnes Sandford, Kathryn Kuhlman, Fr Mike Scanlan, Fr Francis McNutt) insist on the following points:

— Faith is necessary, but those who pray for a cure do not put their trust in their own faith or in any particular gift: 'I do not have faith in my own faith,' says Francis McNutt, 'but faith in Jesus Christ. He is the one who saves and who heals.'

— Faith is necessary, but it is charity that heals. Faith is powerless unless it goes with true compassion, true love for the sufferer.

— Some cures are instantaneous, but most involve a period of convalescence which goes with a slow but progressive re-building of faith.

— The gift of healing in the broader sense is closely allied to the ministry of reconciliation, just as the sacrament of the anointing of the sick is closely allied to the sacrament of penance.

— Not all are healed, but all can find, through praise and the action of grace, the redemptive value of suffering borne and offered for the whole community — and is this not another manifestation of the power of the Spirit?

Translated by Paul Burns

Heinrich Kahlefeld

Jesus as a Therapist

SCHOLARSHIP is newly confident in its ability to use a variety of positive and negative criteria to recognize or recover a considerable quantity of authentic traditions about Jesus. In this atmosphere it seems not out of place to speak of Jesus' therapeutic action. By this, however, we mean not the physical and mental healings which acted as prophetic signs, illuminating and supporting the message of God's imminent rule, but the occasions when the affected person was freed from what were often deep-seated blocks which prevented them from having an open, trusting relationship to God which was a stimulus to action.

I. PRELIMINARIES

1) *Jesus' words and actions were not directed at man's natural and social environment, but at man himself in his relationship to God.*[1]

1.1 The awareness contained in Israel's tradition of man's task in creation, and his obligation to create a just structure of social relations, is taken for granted in the gospel and therefore nowhere forms part of the disciples' instruction.

1.2 When Jesus mentions the prevailing social order and power structures, he does so not to criticize, but merely describes existing conditions in order to draw sharp contrast between them and the structure of the community of the disciples: Mk. 9.35; 10.42-44. Similarly, Jesus does not recognize payment of taxes to the pagan emperor as a religious problem: Mk. 12.12-17.

1.3 The old question of the spread of evil in the world was given

111

new life by the preaching of the imminence of God's rule. Jesus' answer was the parable of the weeds (Mt. 13.24-30). Before the great purge, he says, God will not intervene in world history. Nor does Jesus accept the ancious question of the people who are worried by the murder of the Galilean pilgrims at the sacred moment of sacrifice. Jesus simply repeats his call for repentance (Lk. 13.1-5).

1.4 With regard to man's subordination to the processes of nature and history, we find that while there is an emphasis on inner guidance for the specific path of discipleship and on the transforming power of prayer, nothing is said about 'providence' in the sense of a general guidance of things. The sayings about the sparrows and the hairs of the head (Mt. 10.29; 30 Q) are not completely general, but refer to the situation of the endangered missionaries. Close by is the saying about the Spirit of God which will inspire and embolden the witnesses before courts: Mk. 13.11. Underlying this is the idea that the messenger's master is God himself: Mt. 10.9-10. The clearest text on the subject seems to be Mt. 6.25-33 Q. Again here, however, probably only the little parable about life and food, the body and clothing, is authentic, and verses 26 ff. may have been taken from popular Jewish piety (see Rabbi Simeon ben Eleazar, *Bill*. I, 436). In other words, the disciple's relationship to God does not alter his earthly situation, but by giving him a knowledge of God's nearness and a share in his patience it makes him able to cope with the events of life. Doing without the idea of an ubiquitous providence requires the sober courage of an 'adult'. A therapeutic process is indicated.

II. THE ESCHATOLOGICAL FRAMEWORK AND MAIN EMPHASIS OF JESUS' ACTION

2) *Jesus agrees with the Baptist in announcing the eschatological situation, though for him this is not just a threat but also liberation, not just a penance but also joy.*[2]

2.1 In the older version of the discourse source the Baptist has not yet been 'Christianized' and looks forward to the eschatological judgment. The Q text retained in Lk. 3.7-9 refers to God as the gardener who cuts down the barren fruit tree and throws it into the fire (3.9). The Q version of the saying about the two baptisms also talks about judgment: whoever does not take seriously the baptism of water will have to face the baptism of fire. The judge, this time in the shape of the farmer on the threshing-floor, will separate the chaff from the wheat and burn it (Lk. 3.17 Q).

2.2 Jesus' words move within the same eschatological framework, as the summary in Mk. 1.14-15 makes clear. The description of the content of the message in these verses is fully borne out by such items as the denunciation of Israel (Mt. 11.21-22 Q) and the series of parables about a crucial time, the fig tree (Lk. 13.66 ff), the vigilant householder (Lk. 12.39-40), the clever steward (Lk. 16.1 ff), the watching servants (Lk. 12.35 ff), the wise and foolish virgins (Mt. 25.1-13), and in addition by those which emphasize the seriousness of God's call, such as the parable of the wedding invitation (Lk. 14.16 ff/Mt.).

2.3 Unlike the Baptist's preaching, Jesus' words are a message of joy. Examples are the parable of the wedding guests who feast and do not fast (Mt. 2.19), that of the new patch and the new wine (Mt. 2.21-22), also in the double parable of the treasure in the field and the merchant's peral (Mt. 13.44 ff.). The situation inaugurated by the message of Jesus is summed up in the saying about the blessed witnesses (Mt. 13.16-17).

3) *Within the framework of eschatological expectation Jesus addresses himself to smaller groups in Israel, and in particular to individuals he meets, and confronts them with God's action as a warning or a consolation.*[3]

3.1 Jesus' approach to people is displayed in paradigmatic pericopes such as that of the sinful woman (Lk. 7.36-50) or that of the publican (Lk. 19.1 ff), or in the dialogue with the rich young man (Mk. 10.17 ff.). Even the dramatic presentation of Jesus' sayings, even if in some cases 'ideal scenes' have been constructed, goes back to Jesus.

Jesus' word is related to the particular situation. It takes the form of a dialogue rather than systematic teaching. In each case he is replying to a challenge. Often the scene begins with a provocative act appropriate to the situation, and this is then justified by the utterance: see Mk. 2.15-17; 3.1-5; Lk. 15.1-10.

3.2 Jesus is also aware of the inner state of the other person. In the encounter he recognizes their openness or resistance to God. To develop the one and break down the other is the aim of much of his activity. Whether it can be called therapeutic demands further thought.

III. RESISTANCE AS A RESULT OF MISCONCEIVED ATTEMPTS TO MAKE LIFE SECURE

4) *Jesus sees with concern the human tendency to defend and give content to life with possessions, power and pleasure.*

4.1 The awareness among Christian teachers of Jesus' concern can be seen in the homiletic interpretation of the parable of the sower (Mk. 4.14-20). The choking of the young corn-shoots by the tough thorn-bushes is interpreted as meaning that 'the cares of the world, and the delight in riches, and the desire for other things . . . choke the word'. Care, which cannot open itself to God, wealth, which produces false security, the desire for status and pleasure, all this destroys any relationship with God.

4.2 This insight is the result of the memory of Jesus' concern about the dangers to which men are exposed. Jesus describes the critical position in the parable of 'the farmer who thinks that all his cares have been swept away by a rich harvest (Lk. 12.16-21). The parable is prefaced by a key which sums up its meaning precisely: 'Take heed, and beware of all covetousness; for a man's life does not consist in the abundance of his possessions.' The scene of Jesus' meeting with the rich young man is also expanded by a saying of general application: 'How hard it will be for those who have riches to enter the kingdom of God . . . It is easier for a camel to go through the eye of a needle than for a rich man to enter the kingdom of God' (Mk. 10.23, 25).

4.3 Warnings of this kind are frequent among the authentic sayings. There is no salvation in 'laying up treasures on earth'; laying oneself open to God is the only way to be saved. The message is reinforced with a proverb: 'Where your treasure is, there will your heart be also' (Mt. 6.19-21 Q). The parabolic saying in Mt. 6.25 Q is even more forcible: 'Do not be anxious about your life, what you shall eat or what you shall drink, nor about your body, what you shall put on. Is not life more than food, and the body more than clothing?' The disciple is urged to separate the essential from the accidental and the care that lies at the heart of existence from everyday worries. The saying in 6.33 makes the same point.

4.4 The phenomenon of care is recognized as part of the truth about man. It is rooted in the vulnerability of personal life and is the basis on the human side for a deep relationship with God. The obvious danger for man is that this care, which is a powerful force, instead of being captured and calmed by God, may be left miserably in the world.

IV. RESISTANCE AS A RESULT OF A FALSE IMAGE OF GOD

5) *A prominent characteristic of Jesus is his efforts to bring each person he comes in contact with to a relationship of faith and trust in God.*

5.1 Confrontation with the Lord of grace frees a person from the desperate need to justify himself. The example of the two worshippers in the Temple (Lk. 18.10-14) shows the characteristic Pharisee doctrine of justification. Jesus' judgment (v. 14a) is that it is the sinner, and not the would-be righteous man, who has understood God's freedom with grace. A similar point is made by the parable Lk. 17.7-10.

5.2 Mt. 6.1-6; 16.18, a didactic poem in three sections, is a reminder that the 'jealous God' is not impressed by works of piety if subsidiary motives make them impure. The same message, but in positive form, is contained in the advice not to invite to a feast those who can repay you in kind: God will take account of what did not reach its goal in the world and therefore reached him (Lk. 14.12-14).

5.3 Where God's majesty is taken seriously, fear of earthly power is no longer overwhelming: 'Do not fear those who kill the body, and after that have no more that they can do. But I will warn you whom to fear . . .' (Lk. 12.4 Q).

V. LIBERATION FROM THE YOKE OF THE LAW

6) *The Torah, as the epxression of God's care for Israel, is holy in Jesus' eyes, but he does not understand it as 'Law' to be kept by formal observance. Because of this he shatters observances by provocative acts and opens people's eyes to the living will of God.*

6.1 One point of conflict is the Sabbath rest (Mk. 2.27; 3.4; Lk. 13.14-16); another is the ban on certain foods (Mk. 7.15) Jesus sees the meaning of the 'commandment' as God's devotion to his creature. The criterion of righteousness is not external; it is within the person who has turned to God (Lk. 6.45 Q).

6.2 The attacks on the Pharisaic teaching on the Way now become intelligible. The condemnation of the suppression of God's commandments by the Rabbinic tradition appears three times in the editorial compilation Mk. 7.5-13; 7.8, 9, 13. The saying in Mt. 23.9 warns openly against a doctrinal authority which sets itself up between God and man: 'And call no man your father who is on earth, for you have one Father, who is in heaven.' Mt. has interpreted the warning against the 'leaven of the Pharisees' to mean that the disciples should beware of their corrupting doctrine (Mt. 16.11-12):

6.3 Liberation for a relationship with God creates the sharpest conflict when Jesus brings a person who has been declared sinful out of their isolation through the revelation of rescuing love. Reliable evidence of this is the use of 'friend of sinners' as an insult (Lk. 7.34 Q). Others are the dramatic presentation of the events of Mk. 2.13-17, the marginal note in Lk. 15.1-2, and in particular the group of parables of Jesus which present his attitude as derived from the will of God: Mt. 20.1-16; 21.18 ff; Lk. 15.3-10; 11-32. The protest of the workers of the first hour (Mt. 20.10-14) and that of the elder son (Lk. 15.28-32) is the voice of the pure theory of righteousness, but it meets not only God's sovereignty, but also his unconditional love.

6.4 The guilty man is liberated by the realization that God does not wait for his penance, but himself begins the process of reconciliation because he wants to recover what was lost and because his love never gives up.

VI. THE IMPULSE TO ACTION

7) *The closeness to God enjoyed by the man who has been freed establishes a firm tie to the initiating will of God. This sets in motion a sort of action in which harmony with God and disloyalty to him are each experienced as pleasant or painful.*

7.1 Following the will of God is what discipleship means: see Mk. 3.33; Mt. 6.10; 7.21; 21.33 ff. It is not so much from the commandments that this will can be recognized, as from situations, which make a clear call for action. This is the lesson of the parable of the Samaritan, which is preserved only in Luke (Lk. 10.30-37).

7.2 The old commandment of love is reinterpreted. Its range is extended to include even acts of love to an enemy. Fulfilling it is proclaimed a sign of sonship with God. At the same time, in view of the eschatological judgment, arrogant assessments of other people's relationships with God are rejected (Lk. 6.27-38).

7.3 Commitment to God's cause seems to be the theme of the parable of the talents (Mt. 25.14-30/Lk.). Just as the third servant's fear of the supposed strictness of his master makes him neglect his service, so Jesus' judgment falls on a devotion to the law which is incapable of initiative. Human liberation is completed in action.

Finally a question. It is clear that Jesus starts from the situation of the people he meets and that his discourses in particular have a therapeutic character. But is it sufficient to see the tradition of the discourses as part of the early preaching of Chirst? Should not his work of making people free for a living relationship with God be carried on by the disciples? What would that mean? Does it mean that a dialogue exists today whose aim is the disclosure of the existence promised by God?

Translated by Francis McDonagh

Notes

1   M. Hengel, *War Jesus Revolutionär?* (Stuttgart, 1970). H. Conzelmann, *RGG* III, col. 640: 'Jesus calls for neither the freeing of slaves nor the equalization of property. He declares the poor blessed and in so doing reveals their eschatological situation. But he does not join in the threats against the rich; these too depend on the end. The two groups are urged to direct their attention, not to each other, but to God . . . Jesus makes no call for social revolution and does not foster envy.'

2   W. Trilling, 'Jesus, der Urheber und Vollender des Glaubens', in O. Knoch, F. Messerschmid and A. Zenner, *Das Evangelium auf dem Weg zum Menschen* (Frankfurt, 1973).

3   The relationship between Jesus' primary activity and his eschatological pronouncements is generally summed up in the antithesis 'eschatology and ethics'. In fact, though, it is questionable whether 'ethics' is an accurate

description of Jesus' intentions. H. Schürmann has suggested a distinction between a set of theological and a set of eschatological statements. This prompts the question whether Jesus' actions are adequately covered by the notion of speaking about God. H. Schürmann, 'Das hermeneutische Hautproblem in der Verkündigung Jesu', *Traditionsgeschichtliche Untersuchungen zu den synoptischen Evangelien* (Dusseldorf, 1968).

Mario Rossi

What is Healing?

WE always want to define precisely who is healthy and who is sick, the
state of normality and the state of abnormality, but we also know that
modern science has blurred the outlines round these extremes and it is
not uncommon to hear people speak of balance and imbalance, of
alternating phases and of regressions, even though illness has its own
tangible manifestations and health is accompanied by the outward signs
of well being. Oversimplified classifications enjoy less credibility now
than they once did, because scepticism in their regard has effectively
armed the scientist, and even educated the man in the street, with new
and relevant information, encouraging the idea of a complex interaction between the physical and the psychical self, and external reality:
our history is less readily idealized, and the potential of our gifts is far
greater than the oversimplified classification would suggest. Healing is
built like a bridge on two arches, one of which is composed of the facts,
the other of the possibilities. A vague sense of well-being is no longer
enough to convince us we are healthy, nor ability to adapt to persuade
us that we are psychologically well-adjusted. The fact is that the
possibilities need to be set against a wider background, and we know
that we can be misled by a biochemical change or a feeling of distress,
both of which need to be interpreted: we all have a share in this new
knowledge which enables us to assess the possibilities. Healing could
come within the context of a decision to change, as part of the need or
capacity to reconsider one's psycho-physical self, and not simply
through organ pathology, a fact of life that must be accepted. The facts
can be regarded either as a strait-jacket or as a gift, the potential as a
pre-determined programme or a hope, or else as an opportunity for

118

developing talents and relationships. In this sense, restoration to health could be a sign of the power to break out of a pattern of masochism, of a readiness to keep well without feeling the need to invesnt symptoms, and without resorting to psycho-physical means in order to cause oneself suffering and so pay off something of one's debt to a capricious god. Then again, healing could come as a sign of one's capacity to emerge from a state of regression by living our formerly suppressed anxieties, putting a name to one's inner conflicts and a date to the time of their first appearance. Healing could mean accepting one's limitations simply, without making oneself out to be either incapable of anything or omnipotent. I might add that each of us should be able to look back on at least one period of his life during which he was as healthy as this — one period when he was able to accept totally his own image of himself and his way of functioning, a period in which zest for life had its rightful place, a period when he was in communication both with himself and with others — in order to provide the memory with one realized possibility to which it can refer. Such a process of referring back could remain like a theme tune on the inner background of one's life, very different from that narcissistic taste for self-contemplation and self-love which is nonetheless the self-protective reaction of many people. This period could also be a time for evaluating life as a whole, with all its complexities — which is equivalent to speaking of the ability to rise above a passing depression, of an elan, an energy, which we recognize within ourselves and which can foster our relationship both with ourselves and with others, and which implies participation from the start, free and untroubled by remorse, the chance to feel that one is within the experience and not alongside it.

The opposite to all this is resigned acceptance of the status quo; getting bogged down in a situation which blocks our energies and stems the flow of the inner dynamic, in the anguish that comes from over-concentration on a single memory; or else passive acceptance rather than good use of a physical fact or a conditioned behavioural response against which one puts up an ever unresolved struggle. This clinging to the status quo can give rise to an urgent need for compensations, because one is only aware of oneself as being unbalanced and unhappy, let down by one's own history and makeup, and constantly compelled to weigh up all the pros and cons in order to prove to oneself how badly things are going. In this way every failure compounds one's sense of a battle already lost, a battle that is not even worth fighting as long as the doubt remains, and the doubt does not simply apply to a fixed, static situation, since the threat also comes from past experience, from conflicting desires, and from one's own need to rid oneself of further responsibilities in the future. There are some people who think nothing should ever happen, for whom the history of mankind should stop where their own fears begin: the surrounding walls are mounted by armed sentries for whom everything should simply be labelled 'under guard'. From inertia to pessimism the way is short and it does not take much ingenuity to become a pessimist: for one an unhappy relationship with his mother, for another experience of institutional problems — and there is no doubt that bureaucracies the world over do not have to make much effort to find suitable recruits: where the institution functions as guarantor of the status quo, those people who have most effectively reduced the force of their inner dynamic, the physical and affective included, gather and multiply. Anyone who will not face up to his potential tends to retreat into a safety zone and to set up substitute pleasures which are intended to compensate, usually in a childish enough way, for the reality he has failed to attain. Healing on the other hand is the possibility of reaching deep into the complexities of the real, and to reach a goal a dynamic drive is essential even if it calls for modification of the way in which we satisfy our needs — though of course some of them must be recognized and taken into account: sublimation cannot hope to be a complete success all of the time. Nor can one expect from everyone the kind of sublimation of which only the few are capable without having to pay too high a price or encouraging the growth of neurotic symptoms to compensate for the renunciation.

The fact, however, remains that even the partial liberation (and we almost always speak in terms of the partial) of our porentialities is a sign of hope, an event which involves the future, a recognition of the fact that we are beings who are capable of developing intellectually and affectively. Which means that we all live in varying degrees through periods of static and dynamic balance; and sickness, when it is not fatal, can come as a pause, a time of testing in which to turn and risk a new balance of forces in one's life, to turn and take hold of one's own life, restructuring it, if only for a time, according to a different pattern. Even during such a pause one's relationships are essential, and the call to live can come not so much for our own sake as for that of those we love; death is conceived of as depriving one of one's relationships, as a dramatic, inopportune rupture which comes 'before' giving one a chance to restructure those very relationships. When healing is in prospect, when the anguish of death leaves one, it is as if one were being flooded by a secret joy, a new friendship with things: one finds the courage to undertake some project, set oneself a definite task as a sign of the inner cleansing that has taken place; life becomes an opportunity not to be wasted, a freedom one must not damage. The same thing can happen after a period of anxious depression, after the resolution of a persecution complex, and it seems like a birth, a new beginning, the moment of daybreak.

But the road to recovery often passes through long periods of doubt, indecision, ups and downs, through many vicissitudes during which it is difficult to 'contain' one's hostility and anxiety, one's lack of enthusiasm, the burden of one's difficulties, and any moment in which one feels uncertain about being cured inevitably brings with it a slight − sometimes even appreciable − psychological regression, particularly significant if, as so often happens, the illness itself is a kind of postscript, a consequence of the many emotional upsets and struggles that preceded it and during which one's physical and psychical energies were thrown out of gear, and one's autonomy weakened. Here again it will be a good relationship, a good affective relationship or one involving transference, that will be able to give one back one's courage and one's capacity to react, because apart from reassuring one it will draw one out of one's painful solitude, enabling one to give and to receive, to intervene and communicate, making one sensitive to the message that is being conveyed. It is as if from a confusion of thoughts and feelings there had arisen a confused variety of possibilities which succeed in carrying us on beyond the status quo. Healing begins in the state of fear, and looks for a response at two levels, equally essential, the one techno-scientific, the other transferential. Pharmacological intervention, whether directed to causes or to symptoms, has many excellent features, but it is also susceptible to abuse; the most up-to-date treatment can work wonders, but it can also be no more than superficially or partially effective. Every illness and every potential cure has particular characteristics of its own; but science as such remains a contributory factor, as essential as it is in need of 'humanization' − as does medicine in particular, which from being simple organic medicine should go on to direct itself increasingly to the entire person. If it fails to do so, the doctor is merely using drug therapy as a way of avoiding a treatment of the distress − as when he attacks the disease but does not confront the sick person, intentionally keeping his distance as if to avoid involving himself in that person's history. The psychological sciences, and psychoanalysis in particular, tend to engage the personality at all levels, with all its inner tensions, taking into account different areas of competence related to the biophysical structure and the physiological makeup; because anyone who goes in for psychotherapy is saying in effect: I commit my history to you as a man of science so that you may give that history a chance not to remain sterile; that you may help me to acquire the emotional and intellectual integrity that will enable me to become creative. In this perspective recovery is only the first stage of an agreement to work towards the revitalization of energies that have been lost or else dissipated in pathological defences; the rediscovery of the real or imagined experiences which have constituted the greatest obstacles to our growing, loving and working. The therapist can carry out his work of sympathy and interpretation, his role of zealous traveling companion, only if he has not been afraid of his own distress and difficulties, only if he has had the courage to face his own history, to look at it anew, to relive it and put it back on the right way. A good technique does not necessarily produce a good therapist, however — sympathy, participation and the risk of involvement must be there as the humanizing factor in the relationship: the healing becomes part of the therapist's life, which means that if psychotherapy does not always lead to the cure of a neurosis or of a mental illness, at least it can make a beginning, creating progressively more room for reality. The second stage of psychotherapy is an invitation not to lapse back into a state of withdrawal and exaggerated concentration on one's own fantasies, but to open oneself, instead, 'sympathetically', to the people and affairs of the world. To come to terms with the past is one way of coming to terms with the future, of escaping from the convolutions of narcissism and the abstraction of ideals that serve often enough as a cover-up for that same narcissism, and at the same time of making sure that one releases within oneself energies that are freer and more truly one's own — powers that do not belong to one simply by right, but in order that what is 'given' may ultimately realize its original 'potential'. Healing is therefore a process that goes on as long as one remains 'curable', capable, that is, of undertaking the journey not out of duty, or to avoid danger, or for the sake of occasional compensations, but because one is learning to 'be alive' for the sake of like itself, and that can be very difficult if the society in which one is living does not appreciate 'curable' people, but calls for 'submissive', depressed men, because they are easier to dominate and repress. At one point or another, the road to health cuts not only across one's personal sickness, but across the sickness of society, which are the institutional manifestations of a life that is 'permissive' or 'non-permissive' but never loved. One's partial or potential cure, therefore, is not a process by which simplistic adaptations are made for the gaining of some satisfaction or other: a cure can be unacceptable to a repressive regime or power system which prefers men who are passive and dependent, even to the point where their capacity for passive, dependent regression can go no further. Some prophets are sent, as if of necessity, to die 'outside the city', or in exile, because healing is contagious: it is not by chance that myth can conceal so much distress and so much of the ritual surrounding death, and that schizoid or racist dissociation can give rise to so many persecutions.

So the struggle for healing can work its way through entire populations and therapy becomes the resistance of a people which suffers and nourishes its hope for the next generation. Are the neuroses, the depressions and the manias of peoples curable? We may be living at a time in which we are familiar with many possibilities for individual and group healing, but it is time we turned our attention, together with these healings, to the medical advances of our times, at least if it is not to lapse back into the more serious pathological states of popular depression and governmental hysteria.

Translated by Sarah Fawcett

Antonio Mongillo

Healing

I.

SICKNESS is one of the most distressing conditions. In spite of increasingly ambitious and effective attempts to control it, it is still there, bearing witness to the wound at the heart of existence, to the discrepancy between a man's aspirations and the circumstances in which he is compelled to realize them. Man regards it as a threat to his autonomy and tries to avoid it; he attempts to protect himself against the isolation and powerlessness it brings with it. Yet on the other hand he resists recovery, he does not positively desire it, he does nothing to nourish the courage one needs to live in freedom — the freedom he fears. This ambivalence is aggravated by the fact that individuals, and society as a whole, have difficulty in conquering disease, in protecting themselves from the troubles to which it gives rise, and in finding a satisfactory explanation for it. All this helps to foster the widespread and abiding conviction that sickness and recovery are connected with mysterious forces which influence the human world. As a result, while some people identify sickness with its biological and physiological components, and label recourse to realities of another order as magic, primitive, irrational, others refuse to treat it scientifically and look for healing to the religious or magical 'powers' in which all their confidence is vested. Most of the time attitudes are not so clearly differentiated and oscillate between a recognition of the fact that scientific therapy and religious-magical faith are complementary and an overshadowing of the religious mentality by the scientific or vice versa. One only has to think, for example, of the impressionability of the sick person, his unquestioning confidence in the doctor, in medicines, in technical instruments, in the healing power of drugs, and then of the way in which medico-scientific intervention gets replaced by recourse to faith healers and unconditional obedience and fidelity to whatever they prescribe.

In fact healing is a living reality, not a theoretical one, and it results from the conjunction of a number of elements — scientific, human, religious — all of which are far more active than we realize. The difficulty we have in establishing a balance among them and integrating them into our lives should not prevent us from recognizing their coexistence and their autonomy. Man is composed of differentiated but related levels of being; he is healthy when he breaks through the obstacles which hinder their interaction and begins to harmonize them one with the other.

II.

Generally speaking, religions tackle the problem of sickness and respond to man's desire for healing by means not so much of the explanations they might offer for it as of the forces they bring into play, the perspectives they open up and the hopes they elicit regarding the human condition. They stand as guarantors of the authenticity of the desire for healing, promoting the forces of life and combating those which are destructive.

III.

Confining myself now to Jesus Christ, it seems to me that he gave his main teaching on healing through the fundamental healthiness of his own life and the attitude he assumed towards sick people: he 'converts' them, he draws them out of their state of passive waiting and provokes a change in their attitude to the challenge of life. He directs their attention to other realities, distracts them from themselves and helps them to focus on the fundamentals of the human condition. He warns them that healing is for man, not man for healing (cf. Mk. 2.27), he proclaims the message of the beatitudes (Mt. 5.1 ff), lays down conditions for citizenship of the kingdom of heaven (Mt. 13.1 ff; 25.31-46) and in this way opens up untold perspectives on what life holds for the man who has been healed. A kind of incompatibility exists between Christ and sickness: when he appears the latter disappears. The evangelists, without exception and on many occasions, emphasize the healing power of his presence, of his actions and his words (cf. Mt. 4.24; 8.17; 9.35; 12.15; 14.36; Mk. 1.32-34; 3.10; 6.56; Lk. 4.40 ff, etc.). He does not waste time discussing the origins and nature of the pain and the sickness (Jn. 9.2 ff) or of his healing power (Mt. 9.34; 12.24; Mk. 3.32;

Lk. 11.15 ff), he unravels all the rationalizations which involve even human suffering in the spiralling fight for power and prestige (Mk. 9.38-39; Lk. 9.49-50; 13.10-12), he exposes the defences and the insincerities, and the curiosity inherent in some requests — manifestations of calculation and laziness (Mk. 6.4-5; Lk. 23.8) rather than of openness to life (cf. Jn. 5.45). With an explanation that reveals less than it conceals, but which is, however enigmatic, extremely efficacious, he links sickness with 'the manifestation of the works of God' (Jn. 9.2 ff), retrieves it from its specious and exclusive connection with sin and associates it with a process of growth, with a plan, frequently very mysterious, which man is invited to accept lovingly, not to use as an excuse for attitudes of condemnation or non-involvement. He intervenes where a disease seems to be the bodily expression of the weakness which paralyzes the activity and inventive power of man (blindness, dumbness, deafness, paralysis and so on, see Mt. 15.30 ff), and in so doing proves once again that the healing process does not simply mean regaining one's physical strength. It means embracing a vitality (Lk. 6.19; 8.40), often passed on by means of touch (cf. Mk. 1.41; 3.10; 6.56; 7.33; 8.22, etc.), which restores one to life, to others, and opens one to the Absolute Other; it is a way of life which develops as it liberates the power to love, and thus to further God's plan for men. For Christ, healing means conversion, disease relieved of its anguish, the capacity to face reality and to gauge rightly the forces and tensions of which it is constituted. It is a power which makes something living of the existential solitude in which man learns from experience that all the help he can receive from others is not going to spare him from insecurity, and comes to accept the fundamental difference between his human relationships and his relationship with God, Origin and Lord of his life. Healing can provide no guarantee against death, but it sets one free from the desperate feeling that one is living only to die, and allows one to opt for life even in death. Recovery and liberation thus become synonymous. To be healed is to begin to become capable of accepting, sharing, and making the most of the concrete possibilities of human existence, in anticipation of that fulness of humanity to which we are all called in Christ, not simply on the personal plane, but on the socio-political level as well. Sickness is not only revealed in our rejection of others; it is aggravated also by our being rejected by them, and through our having to live in a society which either does not want to get rid of alienation and estrangement, or else is compelled to put up with them. A healed society guarantees the health of its members, and healthy men make society healthy.

IV.

Merciful love towards men (Mt. 20.34; Mk. 1.4; Lk. 7.13; Jn. 11.35) in fidelity to God who is the God not of the dead but of the living (Mk. 12.27) and opposition to the powers of evil, of which disease is one manifestation, induces Christ to make their sufferings his own (Mt. 8.17; Is. 53.4). His intervention is not magic, it is free and conducive to freedom. He prays to God (Jn. 9.41-42); he acts through his own power (Lk. 5.17), very frequently on the Sabbath, thus provoking sharp reactions (cf. Mt. 12.10; Mk. 3.2; Lk. 6.7; 13.10-17; 14.1; Jn. 5.10; 9.34); he is aware that a power goes out from him (Lk. 6.19; 8.40); he awakens and encourages the desire for healing (Mt. 8.1 ff.; Mk. 1.40 ff.; Lk. 5.12 ff.), involves those who have been cured and asks them to recognize and respect traditional customs (cf. Lk. 17.14; Mk. 1.44), to be grateful (Lk. 17.18), to devote themselves no longer to sinful acts — inauthentic and negative — but to works of righteousness and integrity (Mt. 9.2-8; Jn. 5.14). He requires of the sick person an attitude of openness, or at least an attitude that does not reject life, is receptive to God and his intervention. His demands are summed up in the word *faith* (cf. Mk. 9.23), understood as complete trust, remembrance, hope, commitment. He frequently links forgiveness with healing (Mt. 9.1 ff.; Mk. 21 ff.; Lk. 5.19 ff.; Jn. 5.10), the forgiven man is healed, he becomes capable of taking part in the dialectic of grace and gift.

V.

Christ, who from the time of their first mission, had associated his apostles and disciples with his own power to heal the sick (Mt. 10.1; Mk. 6.13; Lk. 9.1-6), at the moment of their definitive sending out passed on to them in perpetuity the power by which 'they will lay their hands on the sick, who will be healed' (Mk. 16.17 ff). In this way he reveals the power men have at their disposal, in the Plan of God, for the salvation and building up of the human race. He who had healed through a gift from the Father (Lk. 5.17; Jn. 5.19 ff.) involves men in the healing of the sick and shows that God does not act in competition with his creation; he associates it in the full realization of human well-being; in particular, he neither excludes nor actively calls for the contribution of medicine but situates it within the context of those realities which relate to man and have an influence on him. The warning of James (5.14) should be interpreted in this perspective, as should Paul's recognition of the charism of healing (1 Cor. 12.28-30); the faith of the Church, expressed for example in the custom of believers of praying for healing, of cooperating in it, and of welcoming it with intense longing; the example of the apostles who often cure the sick (cf. Acts 3.1-11; 9.32 ff.; 14.8 ff.; 19.11 ff.) and the constant realization of this sign in the history of the Church. Individual men and the community are the depositories of a therapeutic power and are responsible for using it. This revelation puts healing in perspective: it is a human goal and it takes courage to want it, to go after it, releasing one's power to receive and give and participating in the programme of life-building. At the same time it creates an expectancy in man. It arouses in him the awareness that he is called on to accept, to wonder, to think, to live, to desire, to act in a manner compatible with the greatness of the mystery of existence and thus to be spiritually creative.

Man is made to respond to the one who calls him, he acquires meaning when he heeds that call, he falls sick when, through active refusal or incapacity, he does not do what is required of him, does not become what he was made to be. Total response to his existential condition is the premise of salvation. In the Christian vision of life, healing is the fruit of harmony, solidarity, transcendence, it is a process in which God's initiative, man's response, human solidarity and involvement with the world come together.

Translated by Sarah Fawcett

Alfredo Fierro

Does the Christian Religion Have a Therapeutic Function

THE question is to be understood in relation to mental illness. It will remain a question at the end of this article, since I do not believe it is possible to come to a firm conclusion either in the affirmative or in the negative. Not only the question itself, but each of the terms that make it up, taken of its own, is questionable and problematical. To take each in turn:

Therapy — What does this mean? Both the most recent psychiatric theory and its opponents question the very concept of mental illness, and therefore the possibility of healing it, of psychotherapy.

Christian *Religion* — What if Christianity is not a religion, but above all a form of religiosity? Substantial sectors of modern theology would deny that Christianity is principally a religion in the historical phenomenological sense of the word.

Function — A no less discussed and problematical word: does it mean aim, structure, nature efficacy? If not, how does it differ from any of these? The burden of the question whether the Christian religion possesses a therapeutic function varies with the sense in which the word 'function' is understood. To save lengthy conceptual discussion, I propose to take the question here as meaning: do Christian life and faith produce therapeutic results? — which is less ambiguous.

I. REVISION OF PSYCHIATRIC CONCEPTS

The concept of psychiatry, or even more radically, of mental health and illness, stands at something of a crossroads today. For the pre-Freudian, descriptive psychiatry practised in the nineteenth century, the distinction between the mentally well and the mentally sick was very clear. The asylum walls, separating the mad from the sane, were a tangible social support for the supposedly 'scientific' distinction established by psyciatric discourse between sanity and madness or mental illness, which were classified and described as two separate nosological entities. Mental illness was predicated of a subject in the same way as physical illness: one was schizophrenic or a schizophrenic in the same way as one was tubercular or a tubercular case. Freud called this nineteenth-century approach into question. His process view of psychic illness or wholeness, involving a genesis and an economy and dynamic of impulses, made it far more difficult to classify people as either mad or sane. For psychoanalytical theory, rather than the psychically ill or nosological objects of psychiatric theory, there are pathological processes derived from original traumas and causing mental suffering to a greater or lesser degree. But the concept of therapy continues to have a meaningful application.

Today, however, the very notion of therapy is what is questioned by the more critical branches of psychiatry. They see an ideological rationalization underlying traditional psychotherapeutic practice similar to that underlying psychiatric practice in the last century: a pseudo-scientific legitimation, not of the asylum walls any longer, but of the effective marginalization employed by society to protect itself from 'deviant' individuals. These are not now condemned to confinement, but only to schizophrenia. The effects, however, are the same, and so are the pre-suppositions underlying an individualistic psychopathology. Against this, there is increasing evidence that mental illness cannot be completely interpreted or defined without reference to the society that generates it.

This shift from the individual to the social sphere in psycho-pathological analysis takes a wide variety of forms, varying from a (conservative or merely reformist) medicalization of social conflicts to its opposite in the (revolutionary) politicization of individual psychic tensions. In the first instance medicine seeks to extend its jurisdiction to every social anomaly and to prescribe remedies for the collective ills of our time, which are seen as socio-pathological.[1] In the second, only political and social revolution is considered capable of putting an end to a society that produces neurotics by the thousand, and thereby putting the 'couch' psychiatrists out of business.[2] In both instances, the concept of mental illness as such is considerably diminished and well on the way to dissolution.

In view of recent critical revision of the most basic psychiatric concepts, what meaning can attach to the question of the therapeutic effects of relgion? Any serious examination of the question must take this critical revision into account. A brief study such as this has to mention it, bear it in mind, and examine the relationship between Christianity and therapy in the most concrete and least ideological terms possible. Without prejudging the issue of health or sickness, let alone that of mental normality or abnormality, it does seem undeniable that psychic suffering exists. There are people who suffer in their psyche continually and habitually, without each successive wave of suffering being provoked by a new adversity. Can the Christian religion have any beneficial effect on them?

II. THERAPEUTIC EXPERIENCE AND ITS INTERPRETATION

If and how the Christian religion can exercise a mind-healing function is an empirical question patent of an experimental reply, based on the practical experience of practitioners of psychotherapy. It is by its nature not something that can be answered by a theological *a priori* saying what *ought* to happen in the therapeutic application of religion, but a question of fact, subject to empirical proceedings of clarification and verification outside the scope of theology. The reply will depend on results of psychotherapeutic experience with religious patients. The clinical histories of the cures of individual Christians, examined with impartiality devoid of both theological and apologetic prejudice, must provide the cumulative evidence necessary to demonstrate whether the Christian religion contributes to the therapeutic process or not, and if so, how it does in particular cases.

There are difficulties, however, in the way of a completely impartial examination of the religious factor in the healing process. It is difficult for clinical histories to remain entirely free of any trace of interpretation on the part of the psychotherapist, who is bound to bring his own hermeneutical viewpoint to bear on his statement of how the religious factor intervened. This means that there can be no pure objectivity, and that verification of the part played by religious feeling is far from experiential or purely empirical. The theoretically empirical question of 'what happens' during a course of psychotherapy is inevitably bound up with the hermeneutical question implied by the fact that it is the psychotherapist-relator who notes, judges and communicates what has happened. This failing introduces elements of interpretation that bend and organize the empirical material in a pattern no longer based exclusively on 'facts'. The interpretative pattern of these facts is definitely controlled by the religious or irreligious beliefs of the psychotherapist, and also by his criteria of what constitutes religion or Christianity. So it is that after seventy years of experience in psychotherapy, the part played in it by the Christian faith still remains debatable.

So the convictions and world-view of the therapist are bound to intervene in his interpretation of his clinical experience, and his personal attitude to religious feeling will inevitably lead to a positive or negative valuation of it, which in turn will mark and colour the results of his practice. The atheist Freud found difficulty in seeing anything other than a 'universal obsessive neurosis' in religion.[3] Far from attributing therapeutic effects to it, he considered it a pathological manifestation in itself. If his clinical experience had shown him non-neurotic religious elements, it is hard to see how he could have recognized them as being religious. The mythologist and vague theist Jung, on the other hand, held that only conscious appreciation of the symbolical and religious elements held in the collective unconscious of humanity could permit the individual to be himself and free him from his illness. No-one could really be cured without recovering his religious feeling.[4] Finally, the logotherapy of the believer Victor Frankl, however much he considers religious and non-religious experience on the same plane in principle, cannot help taking a positive view of religion. Whilst religion seeks the salvation of the soul, logotherapy seeks no more than its cure, but its questions on the meaning of life interject a religious interpretation which in no way sees religions as collective neuroses.[5]

The psychotherapeutic evidence freest of non-clinical judgment seems to suggest that the Christian religion in fact works in two ways. On the one hand it notes the existence of the so-called 'ecclesiastical neuroses' engendered by an over-strict legalistic moral and religious upbringing, generally imposed by Church schools with parental approval. On the other, it also recognizes the possible healthy and positive contribution made by religious faith in the curative process. This contribution should not be over-valued, however: rather than talk of a psychotherapeutic effect, some therapists prefer to talk of the psycho-hygienic influence of religion.[6] Some point out that, rather than aid the actual healing process or resolve psychic conflicts, religion helps the individual to bear them better. Freud himself admitted that: 'believers seem to enjoy immunity from certain neurotic illnesses, as though acceptance of their general neurosis relieved them of the task of building their own personal neurosis.'[7]

Underlying the diversity of interpretations and even of experiences is a different criterion for deciding what belongs to the religious sphere. The religious factor that generates ecclesiastical neuroses is evidently not the same one that is responsible for psychic hygiene. The two are different levels and elements of what is phenomenologically called 'religion', acting in diametrically opposed directions.

The complexity of religious attitudes and practices shows in the variety of its psychic effects, both good and bad. It is not the task of the psychotherapist to decide precisely what constitutes Christianity, nor to distinguish between what is genuine and what false in it. For him, anyone who claims to be Christian or religious is such, and the verdict that theology would pass on his religion is no concern of his: the superstititions of the scrupulous have as much claim to the title as the faith of the martyrs. So it is impossible to answer the question of whether the Christian religion has a therapeutic function from clinical evidence alone, since this lacks the means and the concern to define what Christianity in its strict sense might be. The question requires an inter-disciplinary reply, and the subject of the question, the Christian religion, and a definition of what is genuinely Christian is the part that belongs to theology. The psychotherapist can contribute the results of his clinical practice on nominally Christian or religious subjects. It is for the theologian to say what is Christian and what is not.

The remainder of this article is intended to be a theological contribution to this interdisciplinary theme, but from the standpoint of a theology understood not as dogmatic wisdom, possessing in advance and for all time a knowledge of the essence of Christianity, but as reasoned and critical discourse on what the Christian community experiences and understands as belonging to it.

III. THEOLOGICAL PREJUDICES

In order to approach the question of the possible therapeutic value of religion from the correct theological standpoint, we must first of all eliminate certain *a priori* suppositions stemming from the imperatives of particular systems of dogmatics, systems that are generally unrealistic in their principles, and therefore not unnaturally equally unrealistic in their conclusions applied to this particular question.

One dogmatic approach holds that the root of mental illness is always, in the final analysis, religious. What the patient is suffering from is basically God, or, more precisely, the absence of God. Sicknesses of the soul would have a secret irreligious essence: where what is God's is not given to him, man cannot reach the fulness of his humanity, nor attain psychic health. Naturally, this would never be stated in such bald terms. It is generally expressed obliquely and through circumlocutions, the most usual being recourse to the concept of anguish, as defined by Kierkegaard — the vertigo of freedom faced with an infinity of choices. This provides an excellent starting-point for a mixture of psychology, existential philosophy and theology. Used in a wandering and imprecise sense, this concept seems to hold good for expressing states of mind in themselves and in relation to the concept of religious salvation. Its imprecision favours the looking-glass approach of taking psychic anguish as a symptom of the yearning for salvation and of alienation from saving grace. Consequently, the Christian faith should leave no room for anguish. So, Hans Urs von Balthasar has allowed himself to write: 'Not only is the Christian excused from this sort of anguish: he has no way into it. If despite this he is neurotic or existentialist, then he lacks Christian truth, and his faith is sick or weak.'[8] So we go back to the old idea that suffering, in this case psychic suffering, is linked to guilt. Since it is not always easy or even possible to establish a causal link between guilt and suffering on the individual level, this link is postulated on the collective level, and one talks of the sin of humanity, making use of the doctrine of original sin to this end.[9] Human faithlessness in general or the faithlessness of the age are made responsible for psychic illness and suffering.

At the opposite extreme is another type of dogmatics that holds faith to be totally apart from the world and its phenomena, and sees Christian existence as a pure state of being in relationship to God, with no bearing on social or psychic processes. This is the dogmatics of dialectical theology, that of Barth in particular, in which grace, the Word of God and faith have no interaction whatsoever with the physical or even the psychological world.[10] In practice, one can hold this last thesis without being a Barthian; it is enough to be a supernaturalist or a dualist. It is not unusual to hear Catholics state, for example, that sanctity is not incompatible with madness: one can be a schizophrenic saint in much the same way as one can be a saint with cancer. Given this double condition of reifying mental illness, relegating it to the level of a malign 'thing' that happens outside the subject, and of conceiving faith or sanctity in a supernaturalist way, sublimely set apart from the things of this world, it is possible to keep religion and mental health in two self-contained spheres, totally devoid of any communication with each other. So Christianity has no relevance to therapy, and mental health has none to faith.

Both these extremes derive from prejudices: the first from a desire to show the healthy relevance of religion, its rootedness in men's hearts and minds; the second from a desire to emphasize the otherness, strangeness and transcendence of faith with respect to the things of this world. The prejudice lies in basing all considerations on the internal logic of either position, without bothering to weigh them against experience or to examine closely how the Christian religion functions in the genesis of psychically healthy personalities. Neither dogmatic position in fact justifies its own conclusions. Both are really unfounded, arbitrary, and so have little bearing on reality and do not make any real contribution to answering our question.

IV. THEOLOGICAL PROPOSALS

An alternative to these two types of dogmatism can be found in a theology capable of a critical approach toward itself and open to illumination from the secular sciences in order the better to form its own anthropological suppositions. The anthropology formed in this way views man as a complex series of mutually interacting structures. The social sphere, the political, the economic, the mental and the symbolic all come to be seen as mutually dependent and active dynamic structures. The symbolic dimension, saturated with religion in general, and in our case with Christianity, acts and reacts dialectically with the rest. There is no space here to justify this concept, not even to develop it,[11] but as stated it does allow is to make some non-arbitrary statements on the pscyhotherapeutic or psycho-hygienic effects of Christian faith.

1) The language of faith has often been expressed in therapeutic terms.[12] The most characteristic of these is 'salvation'. In the Bible the semantic roots of this expression lie in the social and political field, thereby justifying the present-day theology of liberation in its political interpretation of the biblical concept of salvation.[13] Salvation is to heal, cure and restore the integrity of physical and mental life.[14] This authorizes a therapeutic mediation of theological language. There is no such thing as a chemically pure theologal or theological language without any mediations and never has been. When it claims to be so – in Barth, for example – it is in fact still one language mediated by another, biblical language in this case, which in turn utilizes different linguistic mediations in its witness to revelation. Theology in the past has adopted different mediators: cosmology, metaphysics, mysticism, morals, speaking each time the respective language of the cosmos, of being, of spiritual union, of virtue. At present a political mediation prevails, but it should not consider itself exclusive to all others: the mediation of therapy has helped form the language of the Christian faith over the centuries and there is no reason to reject its services now.

2) The therapeutic mediation of the language of faith is meaningful to the extent that it expresses a real interaction between the symbolic-theological make-up of the believing subject and his psycho-dynamic make-up. Here the Christian concept of conversion is relevant: Christian conversion and development of the personality cannot be separated from each other; there can be no mature faith except in a mature personality. Since mental illness appears in connection with blocks and regressions in personal history, the process of conversion should not be alien to the psychotherapeutic process. The two have a mutual incidence on each other. Psychotherapy can have a profound effect on the religious life of the patient, sometimes in the direction of conversion, sometimes in that of a turning away from God. The movement to conversion for its part necessarily exposes any psychic conflicts within the individual and forces him to overcome them. The old

theological dicta on saving grace can find a translation with a specific meaning in individual experience in the shape of the psycho-therapeutic or psycho-hygienic effects of his Christian experience. This interaction between Christian experience or conversion and the genesis of formation of the personality calls into question the psychotherapy that leaves religious problems aside as irrelevant to the healing process, under the pretext of taking a neutral stance toward religion.

3) Religious beliefs and practice can have a healthy effect on a psychopathological state, provided this is not something exterior to the personality, but the personality itself in a particular mode of its being. The fact is that neurosis, for example, is not simply something one *has*, but something one *is*, leaves it open to the possible favourable influence of religion. Precisely because religion stems from the whole person, it relates actively to the events and situations that involve the whole person: this explains its possible use in the treatment of a neurosis, and its total inability, to take the opposite extreme, to cure the wounds sustained in a motor accident. But its influence should not be taken as suggesting a specifically Christian form of therapy, nor as attributing supernatural powers to faith.

4) The Christian religion is a complex whole, made up of dogma, practices, sacraments, prayer, morality, community, social and political activity: it is realized in all of these and consists in none of them taken separately from the rest. On the other hand, these elements take on a different appearance according to the dominant characteristic of one's definition of Christianity: in particular this means concentrating either on the original-evangelical aspect, the historical-traditional or the present-day communitary. Finally, the religion of an individual is made up of an inextricable combination of Christian faith and experience properly so-called, beliefs and practices taken from a purely sociological Christianity (or even from a national Catholicism), and also his own particular superstitions and fantasies. An analysis of the therapeutic effects of the Christian religion has to distinguish between these different elements. It is unlikely, for example, that belief in hell will have the same beneficial effects as belief in God the Father.

The least doubtful therapeutic effects would seem to be attached to the community aspect of Christianity: the mentally sick suffer, in the final analysis, from incommunication, and the ultimate therapy for this has to be a form of communication. It is as a communion or brotherly community that Christianity can show its greatest power as a psychically stabilizing force.

5) The question of the therapeutic effects of the Christian religion needs complementing by that of the possible religious or irreligious effects of psychotherapy. The cure can eliminate overtly religious psychic elements. Theology would hold that any such elements

eliminated as pathological can never be genuinely Christian. The believer must consequently be disposed to psychoanalysis, open to treatment for his 'religion', in the conviction that a correct psychotherapy can never annul what is genuine in his faith but should rather give him the freedom to pick out the genuine elements.

These statements should be understood as theoretical proposals made from the theological standpoint. They are an attempt to define the possible therapeutic effects of the Christian religion starting from Christians' own understanding of their faith. Compared to therapeutic experience, they are hypothetical, so that it is the task of experience to validate or invalidate them. They are also interpretative, however, and this means that it is for theology to decide whether the health-giving or damaging psychic relevance of religion found by the therapist in his clinical practice in fact belongs to the Christian faith or to pseudo-manifestations of it.

Translated by Paul Burns

Notes

1   For a critique of this ideology, v. R. Castel, 'Remarques sur les orientations contemporaines de la psychiatrie', *Présences* 119 (1972/2), pp. 14-24.
2   This thesis caused Wilhelm Reich to leave Freud's circle.
3   'Obsessive acts and religious practices', *Applied Psychoanalysis*.
4   Quoted by E. López Castellón in *Psicología científica y ética actual* (Madrid, 1972), p. 449.
5   V. Frankl, *Man's Search for Meaning* (Boston, 1962).
6   Id., 'Logotherapie und religion', *Psychotherapie und religiose Erfahrung* (Stuttgart, 1965).
7   *The Future of an Illusion.*
8   *Der Christ und die Angst* (Einsiedeln, 1959).
9   K. Rahner and H. Breucha in W. Bitter, ed., *Angst und Shuld in theologischer und psychotherapeutischer Sicht* (Stuttgart, 1962).
10   For the application of Barthian thought to these particular questions, cf. E. Thurneysen, *Die Lehre von der Seelsorge* (Zurich, 1957).
11   Cf. my *La Fe contra el sistema* (Estella, 1972), pp. 67-77.
12   Th. C. Oden, 'Révélation et psychothérapie', *Nouv. Rev. Théol.* 87 (1965), pp. 796 ff.
13   As G. Gutiérrez does for example in his *Liberation Theology*.
14   Cf. Foerster/Fohrer, 'σωζω', *Theol. Wort. z. N. T.*, VII, pp. 990 and 997-8.

CONTRIBUTORS

JEAN-PIERRE JOSSUA, O.P., is Professor of Dogmatic Theology and Rector of the Saulchoir Faculty of Theology, France, and author of various books including *Le salut, Incarnation ou mystère pascal* (Paris, 1967).

PIET SCHOONENBERG, S.J., teaches dogmatic theology at the Catholic University of Nijmegen, the Netherlands. Among his well-known books are *The Christ* (1975) and *Man and Sin* (1972).

KARL RAHNER, S.J., is Professor of Dogmatic Theology and the History of Dogma at the University of Münster, Germany. He is the author of many works of theology and spirituality and the editor of *Sacramentum Mundi*.

YVES CONGAR, O.P., is the author of a number of magisterial works of exegesis and theology, among them *Jesus Christ* (1966) and *Revelation of God* (1968). One of the leaders of the Vatican II theological movement.

LANGDON GILKEY is Professor of Theology at the University of Chicago, USA. Among his published works are *Naming the Whirlwind: The Renewal of God-language* (1969) and *Religion and the Scientific Future* (1970).

BERNARD LONERGAN has been Professor of Theology at various universities, including the Gregorian University, Rome, and Harvard University, Cambridge, Mass., USA. Among his many works are *Insight* (1957) and *Philosophy of God and Theology* (1973).

HANS KÜNG is Professor of Dogmatic and Ecumenical Theology and Director of the Institute for Ecumenical Research at the University of Tübingen, Germany. Among his publications are *The Church* (1968) and *Why Priests?* (1972).

GEORGES COMBET is a Marist and was ordained in 1964. He has studied at Lyons, Paris, Rome and Jerusalem and is working towards his doctorate in general semantics (on the healing narratives in the gospels) at the Ecole Pratique des Hautes Etudes, Paris.

LAURENT FABRE, S.J., was ordained in 1973 and has written a number of articles on spiritual renewal, charismatic prayer and ecumenical renewal for French journals.

HEINRICH KAHLEFELD is Reader in the Didactics of New Testament Proclamation at the German Institute for Catechetics and Homilectics in Munich. Among his published works is an exhaustive exegetical-homiletic commentary on the *Ordo lectionum.*

MARIO VITTORIO ROSSI is a medical psychoanalyst practising in Rome. He has carried out research at the Instituto Superiore di Sanita, at the Institute for Psychoanalysis, and a psychiatric hospital. The author of various articles on psychoanalysis and psychopathology.

ANTONIO DALMAZIO MONGILLO teaches fundamental moral theology at the Università S. Tommaso in Rome and is the National Secretary of the Italian Association for the Study of Morals. The author of various books on faith and morals.

ALFREDO FIERRO is Director of the University Institute of Theology in Madrid. He is qualified in theology, clinical psychology and civil law. He has published several books and articles on theology.